REVELATIONS OF THE ANOINTING

SECOND EDITION

FREQUENCY REVELATOR

Global Destiny Publishing
House (Pty) Ltd

Copyright © 2019 Frequency Revelator.

All rights reserved. No part of this book may be reproduced, stored in a retrieval system or transmitted in any form or by any means, electronic or mechanical, photographic (photocopying), recording or otherwise, without the written permission of the copyright holder.

The author has made every effort to trace and acknowledge sources, resources and individuals. In the event that any images or information has been incorrectly attributed or credited, the author will be pleased to rectify these omissions at the earliest opportunity.

Scripture quotations are all taken from the Holy Bible, the New King James Version (Authorized Version). First published in 1611. Quoted from the KJV Classic Reference Bible, Copyright © 1983 by The Zondervan Corporation

Published by the Author © Global Destiny PublishingHouse,
, Sandton, South Africa

Website: www.globaldestinypublishers.com

Email: frequency.revelator@gmail.com

Phone: 0027622436745/ 0027785416006/0027797921646

Book layout and cover designed by Frequency Revelator for Global Destiny Publishing House

OTHER 50 BOOKS PUBLISHED BY APOSTLE FREQUENCY REVELATOR:

How to Become a Kingdom Millionaire

Deeper Revelations of the Anointing

The Realm of Power to Raise the Dead

How to Operate in the Realm of the Miraculous

The Realm of Glory

New Revelations of Faith

Unveiling the Mystery of Miracle Money

The Prophetic Dimension

The Realm of the Spirit: A Divine Revelation of the Supernatural Realm

The Prophetic Move of the Holy Spirit

The Ministry of Angels in the World Today

Throne Room Prayers: The Power of Praying in the Throne Room

7 Dimensions of the Supernatural Realm

Divine Rights and Privileges of a Believer

Keys to Unlocking the Supernatural

The Dynamics of God's Word

7 Supernatural Dimensions of Financial Prosperity

Spiritual Laws and Principles of the Kingdom

Rain of Revelations Daily Devotional Concordance

Practical Demonstrations of the Anointing

Understanding Times And Seasons In God's Calendar

How To Defeat The Spirit Of Witchcraft

The Practice Of God's Presence

21 Ways Of How To Hear God's Voice Clearly

How To Activate And Fully Exercise The Gifts Of The Spirit

Jehovah Yahweh: Understanding The Different Names of God

The Prophetic Significance Of Gold Dust Silver Stones, Diamonds And Other Precious Stones

Deeper Revelations Of The Five-Fold Ministry

The Anatomy And Physiology Of The Anointing

Understanding Prophetic Dreams And Visions

Deeper Revelations Of The Glory Realm

The Power Of The Apostolic Anointing

The Anointing, The Mantle & The Glory

The Power of Speaking In Tongues

Miracles, Signs And Wonders

Resurrection Power

The Essence of Worship

Rain of Fire

Healing Rains

The Realm Of Love

The Revelation Of Jesus Christ

The Second Coming Of Jesus Christ

CONTENT

Foreword By Prophet Matthew By B. Nuek	8
Aknowledgements	9
Preface: An Introductory Perspective To The Realm Of The Anointing	11
Chapter One: Defining The Anointing From A Divine Revelational Perspective	19
Chapter Two: The Operation Of The Anointing	36
Chapter Three: Dimensions In The Realm Of The Anointing	44
Chapter Four: Devine Qualifications And Credentials For Operating In The Realm Of The Anointing	65
Chapter Five: The Revelational Secrets Behind Moving In Greater Depths Of The Anointing	81
Chapter Six: Dimensions & Depths In The Realm Of The Anointing	109
Chapter Seven: Divine Principles Of Operating In The Realm Of Anointing	124
Chapter Eight: The Levels Of The Anointing	142
Chapter Ten: Limitations Of The Anointing	153
Author's Profile	166

FOREWORD BY PROPHET MATTHEW BY B. NUEK

In retrospect to the Throne Room revelations on the subject of the anointing, encapsulated herein, I have been truly blessed to have a digital copy of this book as I could not wait for a hard copy (which I must have too!). This book is a must-have manual for anyone seeking to minister in the anointing of the mighty Holy Spirit and explode in the demonstration of God's power. This is a very detailed discourse from A to Z on what the anointing is, why the saints of God needs it, how to cultivate its presence, how to guard it, how to operate in it for ministry, when to minister in it, when not to and so much more. I have not come across any other book on this subject as comprehensive as what is written here. There are no stones left unturned and certainly there are no fluff of any kind that would turn the reader away.

Apostle Frequency Revelator not only writes so knowledgeably on this subject but also have applied in real life ministry what he has received. While he mentions his sources of inspiration, much of the content are pure divine revelations! This book is indispensable for any born-again, Spirit-filled saint who has a perennial hunger, unquenchable thirst and insatiable appetite for the manifestation and release of the power of God in its raw form. This work is God-sent for me and certainly for the Body of Christ as God is raising up a strong and mighty army in this end-time generation. If you are a God-chaser and a fire-starter who's eager to spark off the mighty waves of the Holy Spirit revival manifesting the glory of the Son upon the earth, don't wait. Grab a copy today!

(An extract of a Book Reveiw from www.amazon.com)

By Prophet Mathew B. Nuek (New Covenant Life Church, Malaysia)

AKNOWLEDGEMENTS

This Topical compendium is primarily dedicated to the Holy Ghost, who is the author and the finisher of the deep revelations encapsulated in this publication. There is no book in any Christian Library on the subject of the anointing which is as deep and comprehensive as this publication. This insightful, refreshing, profound and biblically sound revelation awakens the believer to the reality of how the anointing of God can be practically demonstrated in any setting whether it's at school, church, home, office or anywhere else. It is chiefly the Holy Ghost who trained me in matters of operating in the realm of the anointing. He has proven to me that when I practically demonstrate the anointing of God, it is actually Him who does the work, hence it is my passion that the reader will see Him throughout the pages of this book and not any man.

I would like to express my deep and unparalleled gratitude to the Generals who are striding at the frontline in the practical demonstration of the anointing of the Holy Spirit; namely, Pastor Benny Hinn of the World Healing Centre Church, Pastor Chris the President of the Believers' Love World International Ministry and Dr. Peter Tan of Eagle Vision Ministry. These men of God have immensely coached me in the direction of moving and operating in the anointing of the Holy Spirit. Dr Peter Tan is one man of God who truly made a difference in my life, for it was under his tutelage that I developed an insatiable appetite and perennial hunger to practically demonstrate the *anointing* and thus, became interested in the practical demonstration of God's power than just preaching about it. Most preachers talk about the anointing and God's power but very few hardly demonstrate it, but Dr Peter Tan challenged me not just to talk about God's word but to practically demonstrate it and produce the results of what it talks about, hence, he became more of a mentor to me than just a minister of the gospel.

Deeper Revelations Of The anonting

I would like to extend my gratitude to my ministry partners for creating a conducive platform and spiritual climate for me to move in greater depths, higher realms and deeper dimensions of the anointing, to shake the nations and touch multitudes around the globe. It is for such a reason that I have been used by God as a vehicle to propagate the new waves of God's anointing to the furthest territories across the globe, to accomplish His divine plans at such a time as this. My thanks also goes to Author House (UK), for making my dream of writing a reality by publishing the first edition of this book, thereby enabling me to fulfil God's dream of propagating the world with the revelations of God's word.

I would like to extend a hand of appreciation to my siblings; Delight (my adorable wife), Nothani (mother), Zenzo, Caspa, Innocent, Kaizer, Sithembiso, Samukelo, Target, Keeper, Colleter, Presence and Anastacia Nkomo, for their love and support in every way. Thanks to my ministry partners and television viewers for being such instrumental in my life. I command the blessings of the Lord to abundantly marinate every sphere of your life with the rain of the anointing in Jesus' Name!

-Apostle Frequency Revelator

PREFACE

In retrospect to the previous edition of this anointed book, which has impacted thousands across the globe and launched multitudes into an arena of divine exploits, it is worth corroborating the divine truth that beyond any shadow of doubt, the *anointing* is such a key and crucial ingredient for the success of any ministry or divine endeavour geared at attaining higher dimensions of excellence and progress across a broad spectrum of Christian faith in these end times. It is for this reason that in this publication, I have made a conscientious effort to decode the divinely coded mysteries on the *anointing* so as to launch multitudes across the globe into the greater depths of the miraculous. This is in view of the divine truth that every sphere of Christian endeavour worldwide is grossly dependent on the *anointing*. This is because no work of ministry can ever be successfully and effectively accomplished in the absence of the anointing. Without the anointing of God's Spirit in us and upon us, Christianity will only be limited to a *"mechanical operation"* devoid of God's life and power. In the context of Biblical literature, the *anointing* is therefore unanimously viewed as the most significant and integral factor that breeds tremendous results of both personal and ministerial growth manifested through the unveiling of Throne Room revelations, practical demonstrations of the undefinable, uncharted and unrecorded miracles, signs and wonders as well as provoking an avalanche of billions of souls across the globe into the Kingdom.

It is worth exploring the divine truth that the world over, the subject of the *anointing* as it relates to the church has aroused considerable interest in Biblical literature and taking into account the nature of the end time season into which we have been ushered, the *anointing*, has undisputedly become such a popular area of divine investigation. Moreover, alarming calls for the church to pay divine meticulous attention to the new waves of the *anointing* released in the end times have grown increasingly louder over last decade than ever before, hence this divine phenomenon has sparked extensive global attention and consequently provoked an unprecedented wave of Biblical research writings on the subject. In essence, the *anointing* has received greater prominence in both classical and contemporary Biblical literature and given the premise that *the greater the anointing, the higher the dimension of supernatural power*, it is generally agreed that tapping into higher realms of the *anointing* is such an inexorably required action in order to realize pertinent church endeavours relating to growth, global impact, proliferation of godly visions as well as the propagation of the gospel of the Lord Jesus Christ to the extreme ends of the world. Moreover, since in the closing times of human history in which we are living now, we are witnessing a mighty outpouring of the Holy Spirit upon all flesh as prophesied by Joel (Joel 2:28), it is highly imperative that we understand in depth what the anointing is, why we need it, how to receive and maintain it, how to impart it upon others as well as how to propagate it to the furthest extremes of the world to fulfil God's purpose. The focal point is to launch believers in the Body of Christ across the globe into greater depths, deeper territories and higher realms of the anointing, hence the title of the book *"Deeper Revelations of the Anointing"* stems from this realisation.

It suffices to assert that the most overworked terminology and Christian vocabulary across a broad spectrum of Christian charismatic cycles is the word *"anointing,"* yet it is one of the subjects that have not been fully comprehended by multitudes of believers as thousands are still sailing their boats through shallow streams of spiritual understanding where the anointing is concerned. Dozens of books have been written and countless messages preached on the subject of the *'anointing'* yet the spiritual landscape of the world remains unsculptured as the masses are still yoked in untold hardship and entangled in a morass of debilitating poverty, sickness and backwardness. In actual fact, it is paradoxical that the *anointing* is preached about, talked about and written about, yet for all the attention the subject is given, it is one of the least understood and least experienced gifts which God has freely bestowed upon humanity and irrevocably bequeathed upon every believer in Christ. It is therefore evident that although enough has been written by others to both record and establish the merits of anointing, there is a different between *talking about the anointing* and *talking the anointing* and the missing element is the depth of revelation of this divine phenomenon. Therefore, this book is not an attempt to capture in these pages the result of what others have done but to present a fresh and provocative revelation of the anointing of the Holy Spirit that will culminate in launching the world into greater depths of the miraculous. With considerable depth, insight, revelation and wisdom, the author has therefore provided an incredible tool for the Body of Christ to tap into greater depths of the anointing to impact the world for Christ. As you inundate and saturate your spirit with revelations encapsulated in this book, you will explode in the demonstration of signs and wonders that will ruffle the feathers of those comfortable with the status quo and dazzle the minds of the sceptics. This writing will therefore function as a blueprint to not only understanding the greater depths of the anointing but also to unveiling the mechanics behind the demonstration of *the new waves of the anointing* which God is unleashing from the Throne Room in this end time season, which marks the conclusion of God's eternal plan for planet earth.

It is essential to unveil the divine truth that no work of ministry can ever be successfully accomplished in the absence of the *anointing*. The world cannot be subdued, generations cannot be impacted, and millions of souls cannot be won to the Kingdom without the *anointing* of God in action. As much as the natural man cannot live without oxygen, the spiritual man cannot live in the absence of the anointing. The anointing is to the spiritual man what oxygen is to the natural man. The greater truth is that it is divinely ordained by God that nothing should be done in the Kingdom without the ingredient of the *anointing*. As a matter of fact Jesus made it imperative for the church to operate in the anointing through His declaration that *when the Holy Spirit has come upon you, you shall receive power* to be His witnesses (Acts 1:8). In this context, the Greek word for *power* is *"dunamis"* which is connected to *the substance of the anointing*. The greater truth is that if ever there is something that the world desperately needs now more than ever before, it is *the anointing*. Metaphorically speaking, the nations of the earth are starving for the anointing of the Holy Spirit. The empty husks of humanism, intellectualism and false religions cannot fill the empty place or alleviate the horrendous plight of humanity. The world is therefore hungry to see Jesus and the demonstration of His power, hence we have been entrusted with the mandate to unleash the *anointing* to emancipate the desperate and degenerating world. Therefore, the key or solution to every problem facing humanity is in the ingredient of the *anointing*. The anointing is the *current church's diet* and *a delicate recipe* for the church to flourish in a hostile world dominated by gross wickedness manifested through untold human hardship, violence and alarming deaths of people all around the world. Therefore, *the anointing* is our most precious possession in living a naturally supernatural life because God's presence is embodied in *the anointing*.

All around the world, many voices across a broad spectrum of Christian faith are increasingly sounding the call for humanity to desperately seek the anointing as an antidote to the debilitating plight facing humanity. This is because it is increasingly becoming more evident that our generation will not experience the fullness of God's blessings, power, miracles, signs and wonders, as well as a bumper harvest of billions of souls across the globe as promised in scripture, without the ingredient of God's *supernatural anointing*. Therefore, God is agitating us, stirring the pot, aggravating us, and allowing us to reach out in faith for all that He has for us in this *last wave of the anointing*.

Deeper Revelations Of The anonting

Prophetically speaking, as I hysterically quivered and trembled under *the anointing* of God's Spirit, to put on record the Throne Room revelations God instructed me in this publication, I heard an audible voice of the Lord saying,

> *"Exponential increase is coming for I have raised My anointing to the third power. Therefore, take a pen and begin to write and decode the divinely coded mysteries on the anointing, for you shall see a greater demonstration of My power in this season than ever before".*

As the seemingly authoritative voice of the Lord throbbed in depths of my spirit and reverberated through the inner most part of my being, I was awakened to a divine consciousness of living in a realm in which it is naturally supernaturally to demonstrate the anointing. It was akin to Paul's divine encounter in which he was caught up to the Third Heaven, whose experience he penned as, *"something inexpressible for man to tell"*. In a similar fashion, this divine experience birthed in me an impetus that provoked an insatiable appetite, perennial hunger and unquenchable thirst to desperately pursue *the anointing* more than ever before. Since then, my faith in God's anointing skyrocketed and it is my daily consciousness to seek new avenues, platforms and opportunities to demonstrate the anointing of the Holy Spirit and I will remain unsatisfied until I experience the fullness of what God longs for us to possess in this new era. It is for this reason that I strongly contend in my writings that operating in greater dimensions of the anointing is *not an option* but *an imperative action* especially in this end time season.

Moreover, despite a myriad of writings on this subject, it has been noted that many of the teachings on the *anointing* in charismatic cycles are purely based on *theological research perspectives* which in most cases are devoid of *deeper revelations* or insights from the Holy Ghost. The difference between *revelation knowledge* and *scriptural knowledge* is that *scriptural knowledge* is based on the diligent study, memorisation and conceptualisation of the scriptures *(logos)* while *revelation knowledge* comes as a supernatural flood of ideas *(rhema)* and nuggets of spiritual truths emanating directly from the realm of the spirit and is given for a specific purpose. Therefore, my solemn intent in this publication is to shine a greater light of truth to dispel the common misconceptions held by thousands of Christians across the globe regarding the divine phenomenon of the *anointing*. For this reason, this book contains a flood of Throne Room revelations that will ignite a blazing flame of fire in your spirit and revolutionise your life forever. It brings you to a melting pot of understanding of the deeper realms of the anointing depths that will cause you to function in an arena of the supernatural which millions probably dream of. This publication is therefore a comprehensive divine approach that seeks to examine the subject of the *anointing* from a holistic revelation perspective. In an endeavour to enhance a significant level of understanding of the subject of the *anointing* of the Holy Spirit, the birthing forth of streams of divine revelations encapsulated in this publication coupled with an optimum combination of both *theoretical* and *practical perspectives* as well as the use of Bible as a major source of reference in all scenarios and cases presented in this writing, is what solidifies, validates and authenticates this publication.

The most common misunderstanding I have observed relating to *the anointing* is the misconstrued notion that God only gives the anointing to a few, select individuals in the body of Christ. This has culminated in a divine scenario in which the masses erroneously presume that only pastors should move or operate in the *realms of the anointing*, hence the tendency to relegate the anointing to a pastoral agenda. This is often punctuated by the erroneous belief that the anointing is a mandate for those who seem to have somehow attained a stratospheric pinnacle of enlightenment in matters of the spirit. This creates a scenario whereby multitudes of believers turn out to be fans of men of God while in the process neglecting their own callings and Heaven-ordained ministries. As a result, many migrate from church to church in search of an *impartation of the anointing*, instead of developing the quality of their spirit to listen to the directive voice of God by themselves. This creates a scenario in which people *chase after the anointing* in the dark which somewhat compromises its integrity as a sacred, valuable and the most precious divine Heavenly substance. Subconsciously, many have been trained and accustomed for the man of God to lay hands on them, hence their faith is still affixed to the hand of the man instead of the hand of God. The other gross misconception is that the *anointing* comes on men and women only for brief moments, after which it mysteriously disappears until another time when it is needed. Such a misconception can culminate in a situation whereby believers unknowingly limit or restrict themselves from tapping into greater depths of *the anointing* by waiting for *the anointing* to manifest only at a particular time rather than *stirring or activating it from within the depths of their spirits* anytime, anywhere and anyhow. In my capacity as an Apostle, I have therefore been given a divine Heavenly mandate to demystify these misconceptions so as to put the concept of the *anointing* in its correct divine perspective.

In view of the above, the greater truth is that *the anointing* is not imparted only to pastors and leaders of the church since God is not a respecter of any persons. The anointing is not just an exclusive preserve for pastors, instead it is a divine legitimate birth right and an irrevocable inheritance of every believer. Secondly, God intends *the anointing* of the Holy Spirit to become an indispensable and integral part of every Christian's life and ministry and not something that comes and disappears mysteriously. Thirdly, *the anointing* is for every believer to demonstrate it, hence it should be a part of your life, no matter who you are or what position you hold in the Body of Christ. Philosophically speaking, the church custodian needs the anointing as much as the pastor needs it. The bus driver and the receptionist need *the anointing*. The nurse at the clinic, the accountant in the office, the police officer in his beat needs to walk in *the anointing*, the vendor in the street, the teacher in the classroom and the mechanic in a garage all need to experience and possess the *precious anointing* of the Holy Spirit if they are to function to the degree God intends them to minister in the Body of Christ. Generally, everybody in the land, right from the President down to the lowest man on earth, needs *the anointing*. The anointing is not a church ideal, merchandise or product; hence should not be confined within the vicinity of church doors and bars but must be publicly demonstrated in the market place, precipitated in the streets, manifested in the offices and propagated in every sphere of human endeavour.

To secure an in-depth understanding of the *anointing,* in terms of the mechanics of how to operate in that grace, you must have a deeper revelation of *Christianity* because the anointing flows from that revelation. The word *Christianity* is derived from the Greek word *"Christ"* which means *"the anointed"*. The Bible unveils a strikingly powerful reality of the spirit, that in our capacity as Christians, we are *"in Christ"* and *"Christ is in us"*. Being in Christ alludes to the fact that we are *"in the Anointed."* Being in the Anointed One, implies that we are already operating in the zone of the *anointing*. Moreover, the Bible unveils the highest revelation of Christianity in the New Testament, which is: *"Christ in me the Hope of Glory"*. This means that Christ (*Who is the anointing*) dwells in us through the Holy Spirit. That means by virtue of us being born again Christians, we already have *the Christ (the anointing)* in us, hence our onus is to unleash and demonstrate that grace from the depths of our spirit, to impact the world for Christ (*the person*). Inevitably, this draws us to a conclusion that anybody who doesn't manifest or demonstrate the anointing is not a genuine Christian because *Christianity* has everything to do with *the anointing*. Figuratively speaking, in the same way a piece of wood has a potential to become a flame until it is ignited, the nature of *the anointing* is such that it needs to be *demonstrated* for the glory of God to be revealed. Contrary to what multitudes of folks presume, *Christianity* is not a religion, a title or an association but a *body of anointed people manifesting the realities of the works of Christ*, which is *the anointing* on earth. By God's Grand Design, it is therefore imperative that anybody who is a Christian should demonstrate *the anointing* of the Holy Spirit. Philosophically speaking, if you are a Christian, that means you are *anointed* and if you are *anointed*, then you need to propagate that anointing to the furthest extremes of the globe on behalf on the Kingdom, impacting nations and the world for Christ by *the anointing*.

Therefore, if ever you want an unprecedented wave of power coupled with measureless volumes of *the anointing* to flood your life and ministry in ways that you have never witnessed before, continue to plunge into the depths of a flood of revelations encapsulated in this book. As you read through this Heaven-ordained anointed book, dozen volumes of *the anointing* shall rain upon you and flood your spirit, saturate you to the brink of full spiritual capacity, catapult you to the highest realms of power, accelerate you to your divine destiny, jettison you to an arena of your manifested destiny by decoding destiny codes and elevate you to the greater depths of God's presence. In this case, you would not have to wait for you to finish reading it so that you can make a prayer for *the anointing* to come. Instead, as you are reading through, you will literally absorb *the anointing* from the pages of this book into your spirit such that results will immediately manifest through a practical display of signs and wonders as *the river of anointing* floods your spirit and oozes out of you to *impact the world* by touching those in your sphere of contact. The reality of the scripture which professes that *out of your belly shall rivers of living waters flow* (John 7:38) shall become a common experience and an order of the day as the *river of the anointing* profusely flows through you to touch multitudes across the globe. In other words, you will receive such a heavy impartation that will put springs in your spirit and catapult you to even greater dimensions in the realm of *the anointing*. Moreover, an unusual anointing will invade the corridors of your inner man, saturate every fibre of your being, and permeate every bone of your body such that the anointing becomes your second nature as it unreservedly oozes out of you whenever you go to subdue the world for Christ.

In a practical sense, the reading of this book will culminate in the following seventh fold spiritual realities: Firstly, it will open your mind to the scriptures and cause you to understand the word of God at a higher level in ways you have never experienced before. Secondly, it will rain a flood of revelations upon your spirit and saturate you with high volumes of *the anointing* to the brink of full spiritual capacity. Thirdly, it will provoke an unprecedented stream flow of God's power for you to move in the realm of the undefinable, uncharted and unrecorded miracles, signs and wonders. Fourthly, it will open financial doors and supernatural opportunities to launch you into the realm of prosperity and abundance. Fifthly, it will catapult you into an unfamiliar realm of the miraculous in which it's naturally supernatural to raise the dead, open the eyes of the blind, raise cripples from wheel chairs and heal incurable illnesses. Sixthly, it will unleash and skyrocket your faith to move in the realm of impossibility than ever before. Lastly, it will propel you into the future, thrust you into the realities of higher dimensions of the Spirit, catapult you into higher realms of glory, jettison you into deeper and unexplored territories of the Glory Realm and elevate you to the depths of God's presence like never before.

Against this background, I therefore urge you to read this book meditatively to allow these divine truths to sink into the depths of your being. Colloquially speaking, sit on the edge of your seat and fasten your seat belt as you walk with the author through this anointed book. This is a man who has an insatiable hunger to see the ushering in of the Kingdom of God through ordinary people with radical faith; people who believe they are cutting-edge world changers because of the *anointing* that they have received from above. My solemn intent is therefore to spearhead a global spiritual awakening that every Christian should demonstrate the *anointing,* to raise a radical generation and unique breed of believers who shall shake this world through a mass demonstration of *the anointing*. Hence, this writing will make it easier for you to launch into greater depths, higher dimensions and deeper realms of the anointing of God in your life.

Conclusively, this publication is therefore a comprehensive topical compendium that systematically provides a divine revelatory perspective on the subject of *the anointing*, in terms of what an *anointing* is, what it actually does, its importance, its origin, reasons for its divine orchestration in the supernatural realm as well as its divine flow and connectivity. It also unveils the rationale behind the *release of the anointing,* divine qualifications and credentials for moving in the *anointing*, the *analogy of the anointing*, divine operation and *inflow of the anointing*, the impact of the *anointing* upon a vessel, how to attract, trigger or provoke the flow of the *anointing* in your life or ministry, the secrets behind tapping into greater depths of the *anointing* as well as the prerequisites and key determinants for moving is higher dimensions of the *anointing*. It further typifies a practical guide to demonstrating *the anointing*, exploring divergent *dimensions of the anointing* and their practical application, dissecting the realm of *new anointing*, as well as expounding on the limitations to operating in higher dimensions of *the anointing*. In a view to enhance a significant level of understanding of the subject of the "*anointing*", this book is essentially divided into two parts; the theoretical section named, *"Deeper Revelations of The Anointing",* and the practical part named, *"Practical Demonstrations of The Anointing"*

CHAPTER ONE

DEFINING THE ANOINTING FROM A DIVINE REVELATIONAL PERSPECTIVE

What Is The Anointing?

Despite its heightened degree of publicity as a divine phenomenon in the realm of God's power, the anointing can be one of those subjective Biblical phrases that can mean different things to different people based on their understanding and interpretation. When someone says, *"That man is anointed"* or *"She is an anointed singer,"* or *"That was an anointed worship set,"* what exactly are they saying? Do they really understand what exactly they are implying? Has it assimilated into the depths of their being what the anointing is all about? This is because not every Christian seem to have caught a clear understanding and revelation of what *'the anointing'* is. It appears that the *anointing* is understood or perceived by different denominations differently, especially in these modern days, whereby almost everything is said to be *anointed*. It is against this background that accurately and comprehensively defining the *anointing* has become a subject of great interest to the author since a conscientious effort has been made in this publication to produce a substantial body of revelations and practical scenarios devoted to understanding the anointing.

It is of paramount significance to unveil the divine truth that while an attempt has been made by various scholars and theologians across a broad spectrum of both Christian classical and charismatic cycles to try and explicate *the anointing,* it has been unanimously observed that many definitions and explanations encapsulated in the description of the anointing suffer limitations of being a one sided, theoretical view which lacks both practical and revelation perspectives. The greater truth is that defining the *anointing* from only a theological perspective does not bring about an in-depth un-

Deeper Revelations Of The anointing

derstanding of the concept because it is not enough *to just talk about a concept.* Instead, it matters most when *one demonstrates it.* Metaphorically speaking, in the same way just one drop of water is not sufficient to cool up the whole engine, a one sided perspective to the description of *the anointing* is not enough to trigger a profound or in-depth understanding of such a broad divine phenomenon. It is therefore highly imperative in our attempt to dissect the subject of the *anointing* that we define it from a comprehensive and holistic perspective by examining it from all angles (*through incorporating both theological, practical and revelational perspectives*). In this regard, *three* critical definitions seem to suffice in the description of the term *anointing:*

Firstly, the anointing is an *impartation* of God's supernatural ability upon an available and yielded vessel to enable it to do His work efficiently and effectively. In other words, it is a divine ability infused upon a vessel to enable it to operate like God on earth. To operate like God means to assume the faculties of God such that you are able to talk as God talks, see as God sees, think as God thinks and act as God acts. Therefore, the anointing is the empowerment for us to live the way Christ desires us to live through demonstrating the Kingdom of Heaven on earth. To be anointed means to be empowered by God to do a particular task, hence metaphorically speaking, the anointing could therefore be best described as *God on flesh doing those things that flesh cannot do.* In other words, it is God doing those things only He can do, and doing them through a flesh and blood, earthly vessel (2 Corinthians 4:7).

Secondly, the anointing is a divine *enablement* of the Holy Ghost geared to equip and empower either an individual or a group of people for service and accomplishment of divine tasks or assignments. In other words, it is the Supernatural enablement manifested by the presence of the Holy Spirit operating upon or through an individual or corporate group of people to produce the works of Jesus. It is God giving insight, power, and enablement through the Spirit to the human vessel in order that he/ she may do this work in a manner that lifts it up beyond simple human efforts and endeavours. In a literal sense, it is the presence of the Holy Spirit being smeared upon someone. It is literally the smearing of the substance of the anointing of the Holy Spirit into our lives that makes us able to do what He wants done *excellently and exceptionally*. It is when the Holy Spirit supernaturally enables you to do something that you cannot take credit for by natural talent or physical means. In other words, it is the grace given by the Holy Spirit that makes an individual a "*superman*" by performing beyond the level of human talent, reasoning, skill, ability and intelligence.

#3

Thirdly, **the anointing is an *endowment* of a spiritual substance upon both a living and non-living object to enable it to perform beyond human and natural limitations.** In this context, to be anointed by God means to be supernaturally endowed with divine assistance to do the appointed task for which God has called you. Therefore, the anointing is that divine energy that comes upon you and separates you from yourself and fills you with His power such that when you speak, it's like God speaking and when you act, it's like God acting and when you look at a situation, it's like God looking through your very own eyes. In other words, it is the overflowing life of Jesus which endows supernatural strength, enabling a person to perform a special task or function in an office he is called and appointed to. Therefore to be anointed by God is not only to be handpicked, but also to be endowed or empowered by Him for the task or position to which He has called you.

KEY AND INTEGRAL ASPECTS OF THE DEFINITION THAT REQUIRES CLARIFICATION.

In an endeavour to establish an in-depth, profound and significant level of understanding of this divine phenomenon it is of paramount importance that three aspects which form the core of the definition of the *anointing* be clarified. The critical or central terminology used in the description of the anointing which requires further clarification is **impartation, enablement and endowment.** This is meant to enhance a solid understanding of certain expressions and terminology that is used in the description of this divine phenomenon of the *anointing*. It is worth admonishing in this regard that it is not my solemn intent to form a doctrine on this subject but to provide revelation guidelines which you could use in a view to fully comprehend the dynamics of this divine phenomenon.

First definition:

*The anointing is an impartation of God's supernatural ability upon a vessel to enable it to do His work efficiently and effectively.

The use of the term "*impartation*" in the description of the anointing implies that it is the Holy Ghost who rubs Himself intimately on a vessel during the process or act of transferring the anointing. In this context, the word "ANOINT" describes the procedure or practice of rubbing or smearing a person or thing, usually with perfumed oil for the purpose of healing,

Deeper Revelations Of The anonting

setting apart, or embalming. The original Hebrew word for *'anointing'* is *'mischah'* which means *'smearing'*. In this sense, the word anoint in the Hebrew language speaks about a rubbing in and an impartation of oil, hence the anointing can strictly be spoken of as an impartation. By the same token, the original Greek word for *'anointing'* is *'chrisma'* which means *'a rubbing in'*. In other words, there is a *'rubbing in'*, a tangible impartation of the substance of the anointing upon a person when he is anointed. In view of the above, the term *impartation* therefore implies that a spiritual transaction has taken place in the supernatural. In other words, something tangible, visible and feel-able has actually been transacted in the spirit. In other words, something tangible has been given, transacted or exchanged in the supernatural realm. There is an undeniable evidence of a tangible impartation of a divine substance that has taken place in the spirit. Therefore, in the same way a man jumps into a pool of water and comes out drenched from the crown of his head to the souls of his feet, it is impossible for one to say that he has received an anointing and not show it because the anointing is a tangible spiritual substance, hence the evidence will always speak for itself.

The optimum usage of the twin concepts of *"efficiency and effectiveness"* in the description of the term *anointing* implies that with the anointing, not only are tasks executed with divine speed and acceleration but with a significant degree of *accuracy, precision and excellence*. The alacrity with which divine tasks are accomplished under the anointing is what makes it an exceptional product in the realm of God's power. This means that with the anointing, what could have taken years to achieve is accomplished in a twinkling of an eye and what could have taken ages to figure out is achieved in a season; what could have taken kilojoules of energy to complete is accomplished with less effort and metaphorically speaking, what could have taken months to conceive is given birth to in a flip of a divine moment. In other words, greater, abundant and humongous work is done quicker, easier and better within a short period of time. This is the *essence of the anointing*. Expressed differently, the anointing could therefore be described as an *impartation* of God's spirit of Love, Wisdom, Power, Riches and Creativity upon men and women all over the world to empower and enable them to complete the task of reaching the world with the gospel of Christ in a view to usher an unprecedented avalanche of billions of souls across the globe into the kingdom of God. Therefore, the anointing is nothing but the very traits of God which He has made available to all mankind so that we can operate more effectively to fulfil the great commission of God. In other words, it is the supernatural dimension of man which reflects God's very nature and characteristics embedded upon humanity.

SECOND DEFINITION:

> *The anointing is a divine enablement of the Holy Ghost geared to equip and empower either an individual or a group of people for service or accomplishment of divine tasks and assignments.*

The term *"enablement"* in the description of the anointing implies that anything *(both living and non-living)* that comes into contact with the Holy Ghost can receive God ability. In other words, it acquires the properties of the spirit realm and grace to perform or function with the faculties of God, thereby operating with Heavenly efficiency. In essence, the anointing can be spoken of as a grace given to a vessel by the Holy Ghost to enable him to accomplish certain divine tasks in a generation. It must therefore be fully understood in this regard that it is the Holy Ghost who administers *(measures, allocates, disseminate)* the anointing upon a vessel. The Holy Ghost is the originator or source of the anointing, hence without the Holy Ghost, there is *no such thing as the anointing* because the anointing is God's lubricated presence that comes by the Holy Spirit. For example, the anointing on Jesus's life came by the Holy Spirit (Luke 4:18; Acts 10:38). It actually took the Holy Spirit to descend upon Him like dove so that He would receive the *anointing*. As a matter of fact, Jesus is called *Christ* because of the *anointing*. It is the anointing that made Him who He was. In other words He was defined by the measure of the *anointing* upon His life. It is for this reason that the anointing is our divine credential and qualification for operating in the realm of the spirit. This is to tell you how critical the manifested presence of the Holy Spirit is in striding into greater depths of the anointing.

It is therefore highly imperative in this regard that a divine correction or perspective of the anointing be ushered to demystify the myths and religious perceptions and misconceptions centred on the subject of the *anointing*. There is a common Christian cliché spoken across a broad spectrum of the Christian faith that God does not look for our *ability*, but *availability* and consequentially many people tend to avail themselves to God and try very hard to do God's work without His ability. On that note, it must therefore be fully comprehended that not only does God wants your availability but He wants you to receive His ability too, which is the anointing. Metaphorically speaking, when God gives you the anointing, He receives the glory in return because the anointing is what manifests His glory, hence the anointing is correspondingly to man what the glory is to God. That is why the Bible says *let the weak say I'm strong* (Joel 3:10). Why? Because in that realm of confession, you are no longer operating using your own ability but God's ability. Therefore, to avail yourself is one side of the story. The other side is to learn to receive His ability (*which is the anointing*) from Him. This is the essence of *the anointing*.

In retrospect to the historical perspective and insight into the phenomenon of the *anointing*, when God created man in the Garden of Eden in His own *image* and *likeness*, God gave man His own characteristics, traits and abilities. In the context of the above revelation, the word *"image"* infers that we look exactly like God while the word *"likeness"* implies that we function exactly like Him. In other words, by virtue of being created in the *likeness* of God, man was *enabled* by God to move in both the realm of the spirit to commune with God and also function in the realm of the natural and interact with animals. This means that when we are anointed, we have the same characteristics and abilities as that of God. Therefore, the anointing in simple terms can be referred to as an enablement from God to man while at the same time, man also inherits the qualities or the ability to impart the anointing that he has to others in his sphere of contact. In other words, the anointing represents the characteristics, traits and abilities of God Himself. It is for this reason that the anointing is such a delicate and precious Heavenly commodity, hence we should be interested in getting more of God's anointing to become more like Him by being transformed into His image and likeness. The good news is that God's anointing is available to every one of us and those who diligently seek it and are willing to use it for the extension of God's Kingdom are the first candidates to be considered as recipients of this amazing divine treasure.

The phrase *"divine assignment"* as specified in the definition of the anointing above implies such tasks as pre-destined callings, offices and divine assignments which God ordained before the foundations of the world such as the work of ministry, manifested in preaching the gospel of the Lord Jesus Christ, salvation of souls, displaying the resurrection power of God through miracles, signs and wonders, ministering to Lord in prayer, healing the sick, deliverance, raising the dead, church planting and establishment, operating the fivefold ministry graces and gifts of the spirit as well as other administrative functions of the Kingdom. Contrary to what multitudes of people presume, not everybody is anointed to be a preacher, although preaching is central to the divine precipitation and furtherance of the gospel to the extreme ends of the word. Instead, others are anointed as Kingdom Millionaires to finance the gospel while some have the anointing for church administration. However, the nature of the assignment varies depending on the level of calling, degree of the anointing manifested and so forth. It must also be expressly understood that not all believers have the same callings and the same measure of the anointing although God deals with all of us justly. Instead, believers have been entrusted with tasks, visions and assignments of various scales. For instance, some are responsible for local, regional, national and global visions, hence the measure of the anointing which an individual can manifest is directly proportional or tantamount to the size of his God-given vision. It is therefore evident that every individual has been called to accomplish a specific divine task in the Kingdom and with it comes a specific measure of the anointing.

THIRD DEFINITION:

The anointing is an endowment of a spiritual substance upon either a living and non-living object or vessel to enable it to perform beyond human or natural limitations.

The term *"endowment"* in the description of the anointing implies a complete synthesis, blending, fusion or infilling of a measureless substance of the anointing, brought through the tidal waves of the spirit, running down or flooding one's spirit as in the case of the anointing poured on Aaron and running down his beard (Psalms 133:1). It describes the way and nature by which the anointing is imparted. It gives us an exact and accurate portrait or picture of how the anointing is poured right from the crown of our heads to the soles of our feet and how the entirety of our being is drenched into the anointing during impartation. Therefore, in its original usage in this context, the word *anoint* means to pour oil upon someone or something as a means of conveying a supernatural blessing and endowment for a task.

The accompanying phrase *"spiritual substance"* in the description of the anointing implies that the anointing is a tangible commodity or a real Heavenly product that is transferred or transacted from the realm of the spirit to the natural realm to enable man to operate with Heavenly efficiency on earth. Therefore, it is a spiritual substance in the sense of its tangibility, feel-ability and visibility when manifested in the natural realm. Moreover, the corresponding term *"vessel or object"* implies that the anointing can be imparted upon anything whether living (*In the case of human beings*) or non-living (*in the case of clothes and handkerchiefs*). It must be expressly understood that the anointing does not only stay on human vessels but upon ministration, it can linger in the air or atmosphere, upon buildings, in the water, on the ground and on any object in the natural realm. The practical demonstration of the anointing through the shadow of Peter in the early church and It's ministration though handkerchiefs taken from Paul's body as well as the bones of Elisha which still retained the anointing to the extent of raising someone from the dead who came into contact with Elisha's bones more than four hundred years after he had died, is an ample evidence of this reality (2 Kings 13:21). The good news is that Jesus has provided the same presence of the Holy Spirit for us in our earthly ministries that He had in His earthly ministry!

TRACING THE ORIGIN AND HISTORICAL BACKGROUND OF THE ANOINTING

Contrary to what some folks in our generation presume, the anointing is not a new Biblical phenomenon. Instead, it is a divine generational phenomenon that has long persisted across thousands of dispensations. It's origin dates back to the early days of the Old Testament whereby God anointed select Individuals to do His work, hence the word *anointing* has been widely used across a broad spectrum of Biblical faith in the Old Testament before it's revelation in the dispensation of the New Testament. The greater truth is that in the Old Testament dispensation, the common layman had no anointing *within* him or *upon* him. This is because the presence of God was kept shut up in the Holy of Holies in the Temple. As a contingent plan, God would anoint the *King, Priest and Prophet* to function in their respective offices although the Holy Spirit wasn't *in* any of them during that dispensation as He is in us in these end times. Moreover, the heightened use of the substance of the anointing oil in the Old Testament, characterised by its creation from a mix of the best spices (*Myrrh, frankincense, Spikenard, Cedar, Hyssop and Virgin Olive oil*) was just a shadow and portrait of the divine spiritual substance of the anointing which God had long prepared in the supernatural realm. Hence, it is worthwhile to put on record the revelation that the anointing originated in the realm of the supernatural first before its manifestation in the natural.

The greater truth is that in every generation, God calls people to occupy specific offices to do His work. In an endeavour to enable them to do His work with a heightened degree of excellence, conscientiousness, Heavenly efficiency and a sense of urgency, He then imparts this special divine substance of the *anointing* upon them. To substantiate this view with reference to ample scriptural evidence, in the Old Testament dispensation, Moses received a *leadership anointing* from God to lead the Israelites to Canaan (Numbers 11: 17). Later, Aaron and his sons received a *priestly anointing* to operate in the office of priesthood (Exodus 30:30; Leviticus 8: 12). To complete the work which Moses had started, Joshua received a *warfare anointing* through the laying on of hands by Moses (Deuteronomy 34:9). Several generations down the line, Saul received a *kingly anointing* to lead Israel in the capacity of a king (1 Samuel 10: 1). Subsequently, David had both a *prophetic, priestly* and *kingly anointing* to be the king over Israel (1 Samuel 16:13). Moreover, God anointed notable prophets like Elijah, Elisha, Jeremiah, and Isaiah with the *prophetic anointing* to do His work in their generation. Jesus was also received a *measureless or overflow anointing* to manifest His Messiah ship (Acts 10: 38) as his arrival on earth marked an end to the Old Testament era. This is what we call *the geonology of the anointing*.

However, the anointing did not end with the Old Testament folks. In the New Testament dispensation, Jesus our role model and benchmark in matters of the spirit was also anointed. To substantiate this fact with reference to scriptural evidence, it is also recorded in Luke 4:14-19 that Jesus returned in the *Power of the Spirit* into Galilee. In the context of this scripture, the phrase *power of the Spirit* speaks of *the anointing*. It is through *the anointing* that Jesus raised the dead, healed the sick, cleansed lepers, walked on water, rebuked storms and cast out devils. Moreover, Apostles such as Paul, Peter, John, Silas and Banarbas were anointed to minister the gospel and through *the anointing*, they moved in greater dimensions of miracles, signs and wonders ever recorded in the history of the Bible. The anointing is what culminated in a catalogue of supernatural acts, chronicled a Book of the Bible called Acts. Moreover, almost one thousand nine hundred years down the line, God raised men and women of God and anointed them to do His work to the extent of raising the dead, just to name but a few, Smith Wigglesworth, Keneth Hagin, Oral Roberts, Billy Graham, Kathrine Kulman, William Brahnam, John Wesley, A. A Allan, Martin Luther King II, John Knox, John G. Lake, Mary Woodworth-Etter, Watchman Nee and many others whole legacy continues to impact and influence the lives of the masses across the globe in our generation.

In our generation, the anointing continues to invade the newer and deeper territories of the world in greater measure as God continues to use men and women who have stepped on the global scene and emerged at the centre of the world stage, striding at the frontline of the end time revival by shaking the world with the *anointing*: Pastor Benny Hinn, Pastor Chris, Dr. Cindy Trim, Dr. Juanita Bynum, Prophet Manasseh Jordan, Pastor Peter Tan, Apostle-Prophet Maphosa and Apostle Frequency Revelator, just to mention but a few. It is therefore evident that the anointing is still such an undeniably critical and highly sought after spiritual substance that continues to make a tremendous and overwhelming impact in the lives of men and women across the globe in this season which marks the conclusion of God's eternal plan on earth. This shall culminate in the launching of the world into even greater depths of the miraculous, characterised by a heightened degree of creative miracles of glory as well as mass resurrection of people from the dead.

Deeper Revelations Of The anonting

THE REVELATIONAL REASONS BEHIND THE

ADMINISTRATION OF THE ANOINTING

Why is the Anointing released by God? For what Purpose is it administered?

There are SEVEN principal reasons given to me by revelation as to why the anointing is given or released from the Heavenly realm upon the masses in the natural realm. Firstly, it must be understood that in the realm of God's power, the anointing is strictly for SERVICE *and* not for personal use, fame, show-off or celebrity purposes. In the natural realm, every product or substance is originally designed to satisfy a specific need. For example, a car was created for transportation purposes and a house for residential purposes. By the same token, the anointing was created as a spiritual substance or divine commodity to enable man to accomplish specific assignments or divine tasks in the Kingdom. This is the *essence of the anointing*. The anointing that is upon you is for service since God anoints you with His Spirit to empower you to do the work He has called you to do. Therefore, the anointing is not given for the vessel it flows through but it is given for the one it flows to. It therefore suffices to adjudicate that the level of anointing you have determines your level of productivity. This implies that you don't need the anointing if you are not doing anything because you get anointed for a mission. It is because of the anointing that you can be like God in the demonstration of power. Note that it is a calling or assignment that comes first then after that, the release of the anointing. Contrary to what some folks think, God does not give someone an anointing first and then later on calls that person for ministry. Instead, God originates with a divine call or assignment, and after that, gives man His ability (*the anointing*), to fulfil the assignment He has called him to accomplish. Therefore, one of the easiest ways of knowing whether someone is called or not is through gauging the level of anointing up his life. In actual fact, the evidence of a calling is the anointing upon a vessel. This is the *benchmark of the anointing* and a universal standard to distinguish between those who are called by God and those who have called themselves, so to speak.

The greater truth is that there is an intricate connection between the *calling* and the *anointing*. When you find your purpose or calling, you have found the anointing. Until you know who you are and what your purpose on earth is, you will not be able to find your anointing because the anointing is given for you to carry out your assignment. Metaphorically speaking, the anointing is like a hidden treasure that is wrapped up in the assignment, hence if you want to unveil it, you need to reap open first the assignment and then you will be able to get it. Strictly speaking, the anointing is given to those who are *"called"* by God to do His will. For example, when God calls someone into a particular office, He anoints them with supernatural power and ability to carry out the functions of that office. When we understand this principle, it becomes easy to recognize those who are called and anointed by God for the office they stand in because they seem to have a supernatural endowment to carry out the functions of that office with ease and excellence. It also becomes easy to recognize when someone is *not* called and anointed to an office because they are *not* able to perform the duties of that office in a manner consistent with the excellence required by the Lord for that office. Against this background, it is therefore important to precautiously admonish that no one should ever attempt to stand in a ministry office without the call of God and the anointing that comes with the office. Not only is it dangerous for the individual personally to attempt to stand in ministry offices if they have not been called and anointed to that office, but it can also bring great harm to the Body of Christ just like what happened to *Aaron and Miriam when they tried to stand in an office that they were not called to by God* (Numbers 12:1-10).

Moreover, the anointing is also given for a *fifth fold* purpose initially unveiled by the Prophet Isaiah in the Old Testament dispensation and latter echoed prophetically by the Lord Jesus Christ in the New Testament dispensation. The prophet Isaiah, looking forward in time by the Spirit of God, saw the One through whom the yoke of Satan's oppression shall be destroyed *because of the anointing* (Isaiah 10:27). To substantiate this revelation with reference to scriptural evidence, Jesus clearly illustrated the purpose of God's anointing upon His life when He made a public declaration or pronunciation of its availability (Luke 4:10-19). In this context, Jesus quoted the scripture of Isaiah 61: 1, where He boldly declared that,

> *The spirit of the Lord God is upon Me, because the Lord has anointed Me to preach good tidings to the poor; He has sent Me to heal the broken hearted, to proclaim liberty to the captives, and opening of the prison to those who are bound; to proclaim the acceptable year of the Lord.*

On the basis of the above mentioned scripture, it is therefore evident that the *fifth fold* purpose of the anointing is *to propagate the world with the gospel of the Lord Jesus, to heal the sick, to destroy the works of darkness and liberate humanity from all entanglement of the web of evil, to command breakthrough and open super-*

natural doors for humanity and to make prophetic declarations in specific seasons. In addition, the purpose of the anointing is also revealed in Isaiah 10:27 where Isaiah declared *that it shall come to pass that on that day the burden shall be uplifted and the yoke destroyed* BY REASON OF THE ANOINTING. This implies that besides the *fifth fold* purpose unveiled by Jesus Christ in Luke 4:10-19, the anointing is also given to break the yoke and chains of evil, so as to activate man towards the fulfilment of their destiny in God and to equip and empower them with power to move in the supernatural.

In view of the above, the fact that Jesus made a public proclamation in Luke 4:18 that *the Spirit of the Lord is upon Him*, tells us that He knew and was divinely conscious of the fact that the anointing was upon Him because you cannot announce what you do not have. In actual fact, He was announcing the purpose or reason for which He has received the *anointing*. He was prophetically proclaiming it to the people using scriptures from the prophet Isaiah that the *anointing* was upon His life for the people. It was therefore left for the people themselves to place a demand on the anointing by faith and make a withdrawal of that anointing into their lives. It is therefore undeniably evident that the anointing is primarily given to preach the gospel, heal the sick, cast out devils, and fulfil God's will on earth. This implies that the anointing is the reason behind the manifestation of miracles, signs and wonders. In the absence of the anointing, the sick are not healed, the captives are not set free, the demonic possessed are not delivered and the dead are not raised. This is the *essence of the anointing*, to show you how expedient it is for you to secure a greater measure of the anointing in this season, to accomplish the said Heaven-ordained tasks.

Jesus is our practical model and quintessential example of how we should operate in the realm of the *anointing*. Without reference to Jesus, the revelation of the phenomenon of the *anointing* will not be understood in depth. In a practical sense, Jesus walked constantly in the *anointing* to the extent that He began His ministry with a *public declaration of the Anointing* (Luke 4:18-19). This is to show you that even Jesus was so grossly dependent on the anointing to do the mighty works He did. That is why Luke records that "*on a certain day, as He was teaching, the power of the Lord was present to heal them*" (Luke 5:17). In the context of this scripture, the phrase "*power of the Lord*" speaks of *the anointing*. That means that even Jesus Himself needed the anointing just like any one of us, to fulfil God's mission on earth. Ideally speaking, when we speak about the greater dimensions of the anointing in which Jesus tapped into during His earthly ministry, some people would want to gravitate to the level of presuming that, it is because He was the Son of God that He was able to launch into the greater depths of the miraculous. And, of course, He was but what they fail to realize is that *He as the Son of*

God was one thing and *He as a person ministering was another thing*. The greater truth is that Jesus did not minister as the Son of God but He ministered as a mere man anointed by the Holy Spirit. If Jesus had been ministering as the Son of God, He wouldn't have needed to be anointed. Or, if He had been ministering as God manifested in the flesh, would God have needed to be anointed? This is to tell you that Jesus also had to be anointed before He could start moving in God's power because He had laid aside His mighty power and glory as the Son of God when He became a man. Although in person He was the Son of God, in power He was not the Son of God while operating in the earthy realm.

To cement this revelation with reference to further scriptural and theological evidence, it is of paramount significance to unveil the divine revelation of the word *"Christ"*. The word *Christ* is a Greek word. Why the English translators failed to translate it in the Bible, I don't know but that failure has cost us a great revelation. The word *Christ* isn't Jesus' last name, as some have erroneously presumed it to be. It is not a title but a word with a very significant meaning. It is a reference to *the Anointed* and *the Anointing* that was on Him and in Him. Christ actually means *anointed*. To anoint is literally *"to pour on, smear all over, or rub into."* This implies that to be anointed of God is to have God poured on, smeared all over, and rubbed onto you. The Anointing of God is God on flesh doing only those things God can do. In the same way, the word *"Christians"* means more than just followers of Jesus. It means *"the anointeds"* This implies that the same yoke-destroying anointing that was on Jesus is available to you. This is because you can't separate the *Anointed* and the *anointing*. If you're in the *Anointed One*, then you're in *the anointing*. This implies that if you're *"in Christ,"* there's an anointing for everything you are called to do, no matter how small or how great the task is. That's what the Apostle Paul meant when he said,

"I can do all things through Christ wwhich strengthens me" (Philippians 4:13).

Notice that he didn't say *"who strengthens me"* but *"which strengthens me"*. *Why?* Because He was not talking about *Christ (the person)*. Instead, he was talking about *Christ (the anointing)*. Sixthly, the anointing is given to bring the glory of God into manifestation. This is its ultimate purpose in the Kingdom. In essence, you get to see the glory of God through the *anointing*. In other words, the anointing is what connects you to the glory of God. God's presence and power are resident in the *anointing*, hence any man of God who taps into the realm of the anointing and manifests miracles, signs and wonders ushers the glory of God on the scene. In essence, the anointing reveals or manifests the glory of God because where the anointing flows,

Deeper Revelations Of The anonting

Christ is glorified. In Acts 10:38, the Bible speaks of *how God anointed Jesus of Nazareth with the Holy Ghost and with power, who went about doing good, and healing all that were oppressed of the devil, for God was with Him.* This tells me that the anointing is our divine credentials for manifesting the realities of the Kingdom of God. This implies that the anointing is what certifies, reinforces, establishes and authenticates God's unwavering supremacy, divine plans, purpose in the light of His creation. In the absence of the anointing, the glory is not revealed. However, some people erroneously presume that the anointing and the glory is one and the same thing. On the other extreme end, some are just so obsessed about the anointing such that in the process, they neglect the glory that brings that anointing. That is why in this end time season, there is an emphasis in the supernatural for a progressive transition from the realm of the anointing to the realm of God's glory and this is what forms the central theme of the end time message. Metaphorically speaking, the anointing is like the light. The light is what manifests the glory of the sun. Without the sun, there is no light and by the same token without the glory, there is no anointing. But it is the light which makes manifest the glory of the sun. In the same manner, it is the anointing that manifests the glory of God.

Lastly, the anointing is given to bring both the realm of the natural and the realm of the supernatural into harmony or synchronisation to function together or collectively to fulfil God's purpose. In this case, the anointing is like a lubricant that is smeared between two rough surfaces so that there is no friction between them. To illustrate this revelation with reference to scriptural evidence, let me take you back into the Garden of Eden where the original man was created. Adam was created a spirit being and he travelled in both realms of existence without any difficulty. Adam could easily move in the realm of the spirit and talk to God and after that he would move back to the natural and engage his animals. To him, moving from the realm of the natural into the realm of the spirit was like moving from this bedroom into the living room. Both the realm of the natural and the realm of the spirit were so intricately connected and interwoven like threads, to fulfil God's purpose. But after the fall of man, both realms of existence were torn apart. Anyone who moved from the realm of the natural into the realm of the spirit became a stranger, vice versa. The rhythm, the harmony and flow of energy which previously connected both these realms was lost and this is the main reason why God says He is going to dissolve the contents of both Heaven and earth and then create a new Heaven and earth because both realms are no longer in harmony as they have been poisoned by the degenerating dictums of the secular world. Therefore, after the fall, man had to struggle to access the supernatural because of the lost divine connection and moving into the supernatural now requires him to pay a price by undertaking certain spiritual exercises such as fasting and praying and waiting on God, yet in the beginning, man would just peep into the spirit without fasting or prayer. Prayer became a means to connect back to God after the fall of man.

The anointing therefore was given to act as a fuel in the realm of the spirit to lubricate the spirit realm so that man can easily travel across both realms of God. To illustrate the disharmony between these two realms of existence, in the realm of the spirit, objects like handkerchiefs, jackets and trees, can float, live and even travel without any attention but in the natural they cannot do that. But when the anointing is imparted upon them, such objects can be given God's ability so that they can function exactly like the objects in the spirit. That is why after Paul transmitted the anointing into his handkerchief, it performed miracles because it acquired God's ability which is the same ability that is given to objects in the realm of the spirit. It is therefore evident that the anointing is what brings both the supernatural and the natural realm to work together in harmony, thus fulfilling God's original master plan and purpose concerning His creation. Now, having caught this revelation, you can no longer play with the anointing because you now know how valuable and expensive it is in fulfilling God's purpose, not only on earth but universally. The anointing is a tangible liquid substance that rains directly from Heaven. No wonder why in this last season, it is visibly manifested in the natural realm and transmuted into supernatural oil, which represents the reality of the tangible substance of the anointing available in Heaven.

THE RATIONALE BEHIND THE CREATIVITY OR DIVINE ORCHESTRATION OF THE ANOINTING OF THE HOLY SPIRIT IN THE REALM OF THE SUPERNATURAL

For what purpose was the Anointing originally created?

It is of paramount significance to unveil the revelation that the original state of man did not need *the anointing* to do God's work because Adam was created a spirit being who had full and unrestricted access to the glory of God and continuously communicated with Him. He had the glory imparted upon him by God, hence he lived just like any other spirit beings or angels. In other words, he lived a life of glory. Everything he did was through the glory of God. It is God's glory that enabled him to move in the realm of the spirit to commune with God and then migrate back to the natural realm to interact with animals and to take care of the Garden of Eden. However, after his fall, man lost the glory and the spiritual connection to God, hence he became a pure biological being and thus needed something to *"enable"* him to connect back to the spirit realm and the glory of God.

There is absolutely nothing which man would have accomplished in this world in the absence of God's glory if God did not release the *anointing*. Unknown to many people, according to God's original purpose for mankind, God never designed man to operate in the realm of *the anointing* but He wanted man to perpetually live in the realm of glory. However, when man lost the glory, he then needed an anointing to reconnect him back to God again. By grace, the anointing was then released as a Heavenly substance to *"enable"* the fallen nature of man to connect with God again. Hence, the anointing is *"God's enablement or ability"* imparted upon the fallen nature of a human vessel in order for him to perform His work with Heavenly efficiency and excellence just like the level at which Adam performed before his fall in the Garden of Eden.

To substantiate the revelation that the anointing was designed for the fallen state of man, there is absolutely no record of angels being anointed in the Bible. Instead, there is a record of angels either receiving, walking or manifesting the glory of God. The anointing was never given to Heaven but it was given to earthly vessels so that they could operate with the faculties of God on earth. This is the major point of difference between the *anointing* and *the glory*. The anointing is *God's ability imparted upon a human vessel* while the glory is *the nature of God imparted upon angels*. It is therefore evident that the anointing is the *"ability of God"* while the glory is the *"nature of God."* The glory is *"who He is"* but the anointing is *"what He does"*. Philosophically speaking, the glory originated with angels while the anointing originated with men. Hence, the anointing is correspondingly to man what the glory is to angels.

However, this revelation does not imply that man should strictly walk in the anointing and not in the glory. Instead, as a vessel created in both the image and likeness of God, man can also access both higher levels of the anointing and higher realms of God's glory. Angels do not carry or bring the anointing to people; the anointing comes through the Holy Ghost. Instead, it is angels who bring forth the glory of God into manifestation in the natural realm. The glory is entrusted to angels while the anointing is entrusted to the Holy Ghost, for humanity in the natural realm. The anointing is such a sacred, unique and a very special divine commodity of Heaven that it takes only the Holy Ghost to personally to administer it upon human vessels. Philosophically speaking, the *"angels administers the glory"* while the *"Holy Ghost personally administers the anointing."* That's why there is no such thing called an *"Angelic Anointing"* but there is such a thing as *"The anointing of the Holy Spirit"*, meaning that it is the Holy Ghost who originates with the anointing, assumes total ownership of this divine substance, administers it and ultimately imparts it upon vessels.

In view of the above, it could therefore be strictly concluded that the anointing regulates the economy of the Kingdom of God in the hands of the Holy Ghost. That is why a man with the anointing can re-create, control, impact and even change the whole world. Consider what the Queen of England had to say concerning the anointed man of God, John Knox: *"I'm afraid of that man's anointing more than all the combined armies of England"*. This is to show you how spiritually dangerous a man with the anointing can be in this world. As a matter of fact, when God sent forth a decree as a warning to the Kings of the earth saying, *"Touch not my anointed ones"*, it's not that He was protecting them from any harm per ser. Rather, He was warning unbelievers of the consequences of tampering with the highly inflammable anointing He had placed upon His servants. The *anatomy* and *physiology* of the anointing unveils the fact that one of the inherent properties of the substance of the anointing is that it is highly inflammable and easily catches or contacts the fire of the Holy Ghost in the realm of the spirit. This is to alert those who toy with the anointing of the repercussions of such a conduct.

CHAPTER TWO

THE DETERMINANTS OF THE DEGREE OF MANIFESTATION AND OPERATION OF THE ANOINTING

Operating in the anointing speaks of understanding the greater, deeper and profound depths of how to flow in the manifestation of the anointing and learning to channel it in a specific direction. It also speaks of learning to flow with the nature and character of manifestation, intricately observing the trend, pattern, and fluctuations of the anointing from meeting to meeting, from place to place, from realm to realm and from one dimension of the spirit to the other. It must be expressly understood that the anointing does not operate in a similar fashion every time. In terms of its operation, there are times when the anointing would generally come upon a congregation in a slow and intermittent fashion depending on the workings of the Holy Ghost. However, there are times when the anointing would just fall upon the whole congregation simultaneously like a cloud of power or heavy rain falling upon the masses. This happened in the upper room (Acts 2:1-4), in the house prayer meeting (Acts 4:31), and in Cornelius' house (Acts 10:44, 45) and it still continues in our meetings today. In such instances, we may call it an *'outpouring'* of the Holy Spirit. Therefore, if you want to understand how the anointing operates, it is of paramount significance that you understand first how the Holy Spirit operates because He is the one who administers the anointing. He is the Divine Orchestrator of the anointing.

DETERMINANTS OF THE OUTFLOW OR DEGREE OF MANIFESTATION OF THE ANOINTING:

Frequency Revelator

How much anointing is able to flow through our lives depends on the conductivity level of those ministered to.

According to the law of electricity, the amount of electricity that can flow through an object to a larger extent depends on how good or bad the conductor is. Hence, in the realm of electricity there are good conductors of electricity and also bad conductors of electivity. For example, under normal circumstances, wood, water and rubber are bad conductors of electricity while steel, zinc and iron are good conductor of electricity. *By the same token, each person in the spiritual realm has a different conductivity level.*
Some people are good conductors of the anointing meaning that the anointing flows easily through them. On the other extreme end, some people are poor conductors of the anointing and such people could stand before the power or the anointing of God in a worship service or meeting and they are touched only a little or not touched at all. There is no scriptural basis for establishing the spirituality of the individual by whether he falls under the power of the Holy Spirit or not. However, those who fall under the power are more yielded and sensitive to God while those who do not are resistive. Such differences in people's conductivity levels could be highly attributable to people's spiritual receptivity, diversity in background, nature, philosophical affiliation, ideological affiliations, belief systems, reasoning capacities, emotional and mental balances, attitude, expectancy levels and other myriad of external factors or influences. Other divergent reasons why some people cannot be touched by the power of God are the unrepentance in the person's life, presence of sin which hinders God's blessings, resistance in one's soul and will to the workings of God, internal blockages present in one's life that are caused by powerful strongholds, distraction in the environment or sphere of contact, wrong concepts that are implanted in one's souls as the power of God has to bypass the barrier to the soul to get to the spirit as well as the spiritual shield put by the enemy in one's mind to doubt and question the genuine move of God.

However, the wonderful thing is that *our spiritual conductivity level can change with time and relationship with God.* If you draw close to God and become more intimate to the Holy Spirit, your conductivity level could reach to hundred percept. For example, Jesus was such a perfect conductor that the power of God flowed through Him a hundred percept. That is one of the reasons why He was able to move in greater dimensions of power, miracles, signs and wonders than anybody else in the Bible. And now that Jesus has declared that *greater things than these shall we do*, it is possible for one to reach the level where he could conduct the power of God a hundred percent like Jesus.

The extent of an outflow or manifestation depends on the intensity, gravity and degree of the anointing present.

This implies that whenever there is a heavy or an unprecedented flow of high voltage of the overflow anointing and a highly anointed minister acts under that spiritual covering to lay hands on you, it is not possible to say that you have received the anointing from him without experiencing some effects. In the realm of the natural, it is not possible to say that one has been baptized in water by immersion but then comes out dry. If you have been baptized in the sea, your hair and body would be wet as an evidence of the immersion. By the same token it is not possible for one to receive the anointing and not show results. The Bible says on a given day, that *power was present to heal and Jesus healed everyone*. The degree of manifestation will determine the amount of the anointing one can receive. The ability of the anointing of God flowing through any substance is dependent on the level of anointing imparted rather than on the materiality of the substance. Moses' rod was transformed into a supernatural rod by the anointing. Surely if the power of God is so great as to transform an old dead wood into a living snake and then into a miracle working rod, then the same power of God can flow through any inanimate object.

However, under the law of Grace, there is an exception to the rule or limitation of the anointing. At times God's will manifested through the law of grace allows the anointing to prevail regardless of people's conductivity levels, expectancy levels or the level of preparedness of the congregation. The anointing just uninterruptedly flows and breaks through like the breaking forth of the waters. Even if people are resting the anointing but because of the gravity, intensity or degree of its manifestation, it breaks forth to flow and touch everybody. According to the laws of electricity, some bad conductors become good conductors at a very high voltage. For example under normal circumstances, water is a bad conductor and will not conduct electricity. However, if the electricity reaches a very high voltage, even water will conduct electricity. In a like manner, when the degree of concentration of God's power is too high, you can have everyone touched by the power of God even those who are resisting or are bad conductors of the anointing.

The flow of anointing depends on the degree of receptivity response of the recipient or congregation.

It is a divine truth that how you receive the anointing will determine how much of it will flow through you. On that note, it must be understood that the outflow or manifestation of the anointing is nothing that comes by choice. You could choose to stop the flow or to yield to the flow. When a minister lays hands and you could deliberately resist Him by re fusing to fall under the power or yield to the spirit of joy, and go down to the floor. Depending on a person's choice and yieldedness, a minister could wave his hands and command the release of the explosive power of God to fill the whole congregation at once and have everyone falling under the power. He can literally anoint the whole congregation just like Moses anointed the whole tabernacle with oil. However, if inside you, you determined that you are not going to respond, the anointing would not work either. Some people think that the Spirit of God will just move and work automatically without any response or decision in you. God honours your freewill. However, you could literally feel a force moving you. In the depth of our hearts, we need to say, *"Yes, I am going to yield to that anointing when Apostle Frequency Revelator prays over me."* When you say yes, the power of God can flow through you. The moment you say no, the power is cut off. Therefore there is an inflow and there is an outflow.

The outflow is controlled by your freewill. You could have the most anointed man of God praying over you but if in your heart, you were reluctant or resistant, you will not be able to receive anything. The problem with most people is that most of the time they have their entire outflow stuck up. When the tears were coming out, they want to dam up the floodgates and quickly get the tissue paper. In every way, we pull out all the stoppers. Then after many years of doing that we ask God, *"Lord, I wonder why I never have your anointing."* God answers, *"Sorry, there is no inflow of the anointing if you do not yield to the anointing and let it outflow."* Therefore, there is no inflow without outflow, it's as simple as that.

The flow of anointing depends on the extent to which the right, conducive atmosphere has been stirred or triggered

It is a greater truth that the anointing of God requires the right atmosphere for it to flow and operate mightily. In the realm of the natural, before it could rain, there are thick heavy clouds that builds up in the atmosphere and until such a time that they are pregnant with rain, they release it on earth. The revelation even concurs with the scripture that if clouds be yee full of rain, they empty themselves on earth (Ecclesiastics 11:3). By the same token, there is a build-up process in the realm of the spirit for the anointing to flow. Sweet and soft music can trigger the flow of the anointing just like in the case of Saul, whenever David would play a tambourine or musical instrument, then anointing would come upon him (1 Samuel 16-20). An intense worship session must not be taken for granted as it is likely to breed a measureless flow of the anointing. It is important that you create a conducive atmosphere of worship to provoke the flow of the anointing. Worship attracts the presence of God and the anointing of God. Worship creates a throne for God to sit upon on this earth (Psalms 22:3). God inhabits our praises. And when God comes, the anointing comes. Paul and Silas had been obedient to God. They had seen the Macedonian vision, crossed the sea, preached the gospel, cast out a devil and finally landed in jail in Philippi (Acts 16:23,24). At midnight, with their feet fastened and their hands bleeding, they worshipped God. God released a mighty anointing upon them that shook open the whole prison. The Bible calls it an earthquake (Acts 16:25,26). Figuratively speaking, even the earth was about to fall under the power when the principle of worship was activated.

It is therefore important that we create an atmosphere of the *Word and prayer*. The only instrument that will tune our faith to move in the anointing is the Word of God. The word of God contains life – *'zoe'* life, God's life (Hebrews 4:12). As we meditate and digest the Word of God into our hearts, more of the life of God is transmitted into us. If the Word contains life, then more Word means more life. Jesus wants us to have an abundant life (John 10:10). The seed of God's life which we received when we were born again, needs to grow and be nurtured (1 John 3:9). We function in the gifts in proportion to our faith. Prayer would include prayer in tongues which energizes us and edifies us (1 Corinthians 14:4). Paul said that he spoke in tongues more than all the Corinthians (1 Corinthians 14:18). If the Corinthians spoke so much in tongues that they misused it, and Paul said that he prayed in tongues more than them, just imagine how many hours Paul must have spent praying in tongues. The apostles gave themselves to the Word and prayer (Acts 6:4). The church had additions of souls up to chapter five of Acts (Acts 2:41, 47; 5:14). In Acts 6:1, the disciples were multiplying. But after the deaconship was organized and the apostles gave themselves to the ministry of the Word and prayer, they greatly multiplied (Acts 6:7). Any minister of God who wants to increase his anointing should discipline himself from church activities and then give himself wholly to prayer and the ministry of the Word. An application of all these seven principles will increase the anointing upon your life.

The flow of anointing depends on the degree of yieldedness of the minister.

Just like the recipients, a minister also has a tremendous influence on the extent to which the anointing can flow and touch the congregation. God uses the spirit of a minister to touch or bless the congregation, hence the anointing flows through the minister to the rest of the congregation. Therefore, when standing at the stage to minister to people, a minister can decide whether to allow the anointing to flow out to the people or not. In essence, the minister controls the outflow. *The remote control of the anointing is in his hands* because the degree of flow of the anointing is dependent on him. Moreover, the amount of blessings to be appropriated through the congregation is dependent on him because the keys to unlock and breakthrough into the blessings of God are in his hands . If in a meeting or worship service a minister senses the flow of the Lord's sweet anointing manifested through the spirit of joy, he can either yield to it and release it by laughing it out or make a decision to hold it back. If a minister decides to hold back the experience because of what others will think of him or because he wants to preach the word quickly, he loses the anointing and puts the whole congregation at risk of losing God's blessings. A minister who is not sensitive or receptive like that to the anointing wreaks havoc in the spirit because he robs God of His anointing and deprives the masses from accessing the blessings of God. The Spirit would have come on him and wanted to flow out through him to touch the congregation but he made a decision to stop the flow. Hence, as he did not yield to the outflow of the anointing, there is no inflow of more anointing into him.

It must therefore be understood that *there is no more inflow of God's anointing into your life if you keep resisting the outflow of an anointing from God* because it is only those who are pliable to the Lord who receive a lot of things from the Lord. It is evident therefore that the amount of outflow you allow will limit the amount of inflow you let in. There must be an outflow before the inflow. If there is no sort of release in you, then there is no inflow coming from Him. *Unless there is an outflow there is no inflow.* Every time you allow the outflow with the inflow coming in, the ministry changes through greater anointing.

The flow of anointing depends on the Presence and degree of manifestation of the Holy Ghost

Deeper Revelations Of The anonting

It must be understood expressly that the Holy Ghost is the source and originator of the anointing because He is the one who imparts or intimately rubs the anointing upon a vessel, hence we need to rely on him for the supply and flow of the anointing during ministerial sessions. The presence of the Holy Ghost is such a vital key to unlocking the supernatural and breaking forth into the unlimited and measureless depths of the anointing. The Holy Ghost connects the place of meeting with the heavens and attracts all heavenly substances, creatures, beings, to work on behalf of the people. It is actually the Holy Ghost who brings angels because angels ride of the winds of the Holy Ghost to perform ministerial tasks. The Holy Ghost opens heavens and the floodgates of heaven to let the anointing run down from the centre of the throne room, break forth into rivers and streams and flow down into the place of the meeting. Just like angels impregnates and saturates the atmosphere with God's glory, the Holy Ghost changes the spiritual climate of the place, and make it pregnant with the power of God and provoking not only the anointing but the mantle, the glory and the power of God to flow. Breakthroughs come by the way of the Holy Ghost. As He moves, He crushes and brings down every resistance in your way to open alarming doors, avenues into abundance, prosperity, increase and divine revelation.

I have experienced it in my own ministry that working with the Holy Ghost breeds unfathomable results when it comes to matters of moving in greater dimensions of the anointing. At times during the session of demonstration of the anointing, before I could even stretch out my hands towards the congregation, they would already be falling under the power in multitudes and I can literally see an invisible hand touching their spirits with power. What people only see is the multitudes falling under the power but behind scenes is the mighty hand of the Holy Ghost touching, lifting, pruning, restoring, healing and liberating souls. It must therefore be understood that in the absence of the Holy Ghost, there is no such thing as the anointing, just like without clouds there is no rain, hence we need to be more sensitive to His presence than anything else.

The flow of anointing depends on the degree of angelic activity in the realm of the spirit

Angels work hand in glove with the Holy Ghost because where the Holy Ghost is, angels are there also because they are always on standby, waiting to act on God's word and carry God's plans. This is evident in Acts 8:26,29 whereby the angel of the Lord spoke to Philip saying, *"Arise and go to the South, along the road which goes down from Jerusalem to Gaza to meet an Ethiopian eunuch"*. As he took that step if faith, this time the Holy Spirit spoke to him in verse 28 and said, *"Go near and overtake the chariot"*. This is to tell you that angels and the Holy Ghost work hand in glove to fulfil God's purpose. The presence of angels during ministerial sessions is therefore such a divine recipe to the flow of God's glory. Angels clears the atmosphere of any demonic traffic or interception thereby breeding a highly pregnant and conducive atmosphere for the uninterrupted flow of the anointing. Moreover, angels are involved in spiritual activities such as impartation of divine spiritual substances that facilitates or lubricates the flow of the anointing. They also open doors and opportunities for people, bring them out of the cages, break the chains of bondage and bring forth the answers to prayers.

The flow of anointing depends on the needs of the congregation

The next thing to understand in moving in the anointing is that the anointing will manifest according to the needs present in a meeting. God well go to the extent of defying natural laws if a demand is placed on the Heavens' Power House for the release of power, based on need. That is why He says that *we must come boldly before the throne of grace to obtain mercy to help us in times of need*. For example, God will not manifest an evangelistic anointing to win souls if all who are present are already born again. Neither would there be a manifestation of healing anointing if nobody needs healing. It is a skill to learn to be obedient to the level and type of anointing manifesting. It takes self-control not to do things that God did not ask us to do. Sometimes God has sent me to a meeting and allowed me to function only in the teaching anointing. After teaching, I would then close the meeting and if there was anyone who needed ministry, I would minister by laying hands and not through a manifested anointing. This takes self-control because I enjoy moving in a demonstrative anointing and operating in the gifts of the Holy Spirit. We have to learn to be obedient both to what He says as well as to what He doesn't say.

CHAPTER THREE

DIMENSIONS IN THE REALM OF THE ANOINTING

The Anointing Within And Anointing Upon A Vessel

It is of paramount significance to unveil the divine truth that the anointing serves a dual purpose in our walk with God. To be precise, there are two main dimensions in the realm of the anointing. These are the *anointing upon* and the *anointing within* a vessel. These twin concepts of anointing *within* and *upon* are not just Christian clichés as some might presume it to be but are nuggets of divine biblical revelations which are used to describe the character of manifestation of the anointing in humanity. These were expressly unveiled by the Lord Jesus when He declared in John 14:17 that,

> *Even the Spirit of truth, whom the world cannot receive, because it neither sees Him nor knows Him; you know Him, for He dwells* WITHIN YOU *and will be* WITH YOU.

In the context of this scripture, the phrase *He dwells within you* speaks of (*the anointing within*), while the phrase *He shall be with you* speaks of (*the anointing upon*). If the anointing were to operate from within our spirits only, there would be limitations in terms of the broader scope, sphere of influence and impact we can make in this world. By the same token, if the anointing were to operate from outside our bodies only, there would be even greater limitations arising from our mortal bodies. Therefore God saw it fit that He inculcates the anointing in humanity is such a way that holistically covers both the *internal* and *external* faculties of man.

The first realm or dimension in the anointing is called *the anointing upon a vessel*. This was the first dimension of the anointing that was given to humanity during the Old Testament dispensation prior to them receiving an *anointing* within, after the arrival of the Holy Ghost in the earthly realm. To cement this revelation with reference to scriptural evidence, the notion of the *anointing upon* stems from Isaiah 61:1 whereby Jesus echoed the words of Prophet Isaiah, and made a public prophetic declaration that, *"The Spirit of the* LORD *is* UPON ME, *for He has anointed me to preach the good news to the poor."* This famous portion of Scripture was prophetically speaking of the coming Messiah. When Jesus declared that the Spirit is upon him, he spoke about the *anointing upon* which had rested upon Him during His baptism by John. Moreover, concerning the anointing upon, Isaiah prophesied that

"As for Me," says the LORD, *"this is My covenant with them: My Spirit who is* UPON YOU, *and My words which I have put in your mouth, shall not depart from your mouth, nor from the mouth of your descendants, nor from the mouth of your descendants' descendants," says the* LORD, *"from this time and forevermore."* (Isaiah 59:16-21 NKJV).

This implies that operating in the *anointing upon* is a covenant alignment issue which God has ordained for all of His children to partake of.

The anointing upon is for service. It is given to perform certain operations and manifestations of the Spirit. It breeds greater miracles, signs and wonders. The anointing upon is a mantle of power that God puts upon His people. It is like a jacket or covering that comes upon or rests upon an individual to empower him to do a particular task. This is because there are special tasks that require an anointing or unction from God to perform. John the Baptist saw the Spirit descending from heaven like a dove and remaining *upon Jesus* (John 1:32). It was after this anointing of power that we read about miracles happening through Jesus' ministry. Therefore, beyond any reasonable doubt, we can conclude that the works of Jesus, His teaching, healing and deliverance ministries, were the result of the anointing *upon him*. The anointing upon operates like showers of rain which falls upon everyone. However, those who are well cultivated enough will be in a better position to absorb the anointing than those who are not cultivated.

The Bible records in Matthew 10:1 that *Jesus laid hands on His disciples and sent them all out two by two to cast out demons and heal the sick.* How did they do it when they were not born again yet? Even the prophets of the Old Testament prophesised and demonstrated the power of God. Nobody could be born again until Jesus has resurrected. How did they perform the miracles? The answer is simple. It was by the anointing of the Holy Spirit UPON

Deeper Revelations Of The anonting

them. The Old Testament people were not born again and therefore they had the *anointing upon*. This is how prophets prophesied, moved and demonstrated the power of God. That was how the disciples did the work of Jesus Christ before He was crucified and resurrected. They did it by the anointing transferred to them by Jesus through the *anointing UPON*. The great men of the bible who functioned in the realm of the miraculous like Elijah, Elisha and Moses did it through the *anointing UPON*. Therefore, the secret to moving in greater dimensions of power, miracles, signs and wonders is the anointing upon.

However, despite the fact that one is highly anointed, it does not mean you will operate in the anointing everywhere you go. The *anointing upon* has restrictions, hence does not operate twenty-four hours. When the anointing upon is not functional in your life, it will be lifted off you. It will not be upon you all the time. The anointing upon does not remain permanently in your life. When the work is over that it has come to perform, the anointing is lifted off. This is because if the anointing is upon you all the time, you cannot sleep but the anointing within you can operate 24 hours without any side effects. The anointing doesn't remain on you in manifestation, because you'd wear out physically. You couldn't stand it; our bodies are still mortal and can't stand much of electricity. It's like getting hold of a live electric wire, you couldn't hold on to it forever.

The reason Jesus could have the Spirit without measure is because His body was not mortal. Kenneth Hagin says he had such a strong anointing upon him that he vibrated and was shaken physically under it to the extent that even his eyeballs jumped. He had such a strong anointing upon him that at times he couldn't even see the crowd. The crowd would think he was was looking right at them, yet he didn't even know they were there, for he was over in this other realm. He continues to say that sometimes he would be sitting in the living room at night, talking to his wife, and when he gets up to go to bed and steps into the bedroom, it's as if he had stepped into a room full of glory. The anointing would just be all over him such that he could hardly stand it. At times he would say, *'Lord, turn it off. I can't take any more.'"*

But there is another realm called *anointing within a vessel*. Jesus told His disciples, *"And I will pray the Father, and he shall give you another Comforter, that he may abide with you for ever; Even the Spirit of truth... for He dwelleth* WITH *you, and shall be* IN *you"* (John 14:16,17). In the context of this scripture, when Jesus proclaimed that one day the Holy Spirit is going to be *in you*, He actually spoke about the *anointing within*. Moreover, John said *but you have an anointing from the Holy one and you know all things* (1 John 2:20 NKJV). This is the *anointing within* which he spoke about which gives you supernatural knowledge and spiritual revelation. This implies that we don't need to hustle or wander about from church to church searching for the anointing or bargaining to be in the company of other anointed people in order to experience the anointing. Instead, the anointing *"abides"* or *dwells in us* and not just with or on us. The Holy Spirit and the anointing is an internal and not an external experience or possession. To substantiate this revelation with further scriptural evidence, John continues to assert in 1 John 2: 27, that,

But the ANOINTING *which you have received of him abides* IN *you, and you need not that any man teach you: but as the same* ANOINTING *teaches you of all things, and is truth, and is no lie, and even as it hath taught you, you shall abide in him..*

In the context of this scripture, he spoke about this *anointing within*. This implies that every believer has an anointing—an unction—that abides within him, because the Holy Spirit comes in us at *New Birth*. Therefore the *anointing within* is that inward witness which works like a spiritual sensation in our spirit man telling us whether something is right or wrong. This capacity to perceive rightness or wrongness is a working of the believer's anointing. Note that the phrase, *"you need not that any man teach you"*, doesn't mean that God hasn't set teachers in the Church. That doesn't mean we don't need teachers at all because the Holy Spirit will not contradict Himself.

This is because some have taken this scripture out of context and misused it to imply that we do not need instructors or teachers. However, Jesus is the head of the church and He established the five ministry offices as gifts to the church. The ministry office of the teacher is one of the five offices mentioned in Ephesians the fourth chapter. So, we need teachers. To reject the biblical ministry of the teacher is to reject a precious gift from God. In the context of the above mentioned scripture, the meaning of the original Greek word for *"teach"* is the same as that of the word *"inform"*, which means to give *supernatural or revelational knowledge*. Therefore, what John is simply emphasizing here is *supernatural knowledge* which comes through revelation that we have the same anointing of the Holy Spirit that Jesus had and this anointing is within us to teach us all things, to help us gain supernatural knowledge concerning our lives, decisions we ought to take, how to do certain things and so forth. Without the anointing of the Holy Spirit, there is no understanding, knowledge or revelation. Therefore, the spirit of revelation is released through this anointing of the Holy Spirit inside of us so that we are able to understand things supernaturally even without anybody telling them to us. This implies that it is no longer necessary for believers to be tossed to and from like wind, running around looking for prophets to prophesy what the future holds for them, what direction they should take in life because the *anointing within* them gives them *supernatural knowledge* of all things. That is why Paul prayed that we would have the spirit of wisdom and revelation in the knowledge of Him.

Moreover, the *anointing within* helps you to *know all things*. In the context of this revelation, the phrase *"know all things"* speaks of *supernatural revelation*. It incorporates anything- any situation, circumstance or phenomenon which one might want to know both in the natural and spirit realm. Therefore, with the *anointing within*, you cannot fall short of any knowledge, whether it's about science, business, angels, God or anything. It must be expressly understood in this regard that in the realm of the spirit, things are not *learnt* but they are *revealed*. Hence, the *anointing within* helps us to unveil and know things in the supernatural and transfer that knowledge from the supernatural into the physical realm. Therefore, the more sensitive a person becomes to the anointing within, the more success they will have in making the right decisions in life. We should use our brain and utilize the best of our mental abilities. However, the anointing resides within your spirit, not within your physical brain. Yes, the anointing of God certainly affects the brain which influences us to think godly thoughts. But some decisions we have to make in life go beyond the ability of one's brain to solve. Decisions concerning *Who to marry? Where to work? Where to go to church? What colour to paint the house?* Can be best handled by the anointing within you. The answer to these types of questions should be measured through the anointing that resides within us. Other questions such as, *"Was that prophecy that person gave me from God, or not?"* or, *"How do I know if God has called me to the ministry?"* The Holy Spirit will guide us through the anointing that God has placed within us. There's no need to be in the dark when it comes to knowing God's will and purpose. Let the *anointing within* you help settle the perplexing questions and choices you face. You can always trust the anointing of the Holy Spirit that abides within you to point you in the right direction. The better developed you become to recognizing the inward anointing; the greater will be your ability to carry the glory of God.

I recall vividly the day I was supposed to go and write my Final Honours exams. In the previous weeks, I had been running around busy preaching the word of God in high schools hence, I did not have time to study for the exam. It happened that on the day I was supposed to write the exam, I woke up early in the morning, took my notes and asked the Holy spirit to show me the exact questions which were coming in the exams Since I did not have natural knowledge concerning what is in the test, I had to tap into my inner resource, the *anointing within,* because the bible says through it, *I know all things*. It happened that through the *anointing within,* all the questions which were coming in the exam were revealed to me together with their typical answers hence, I started studying only those questions and guess what, when I got into the exam room, I found that the exam consisted only of those questions which had been revealed to me. I broke a record by getting a 95% in that exam to the extent that even the Professor was so shocked as to how I obtained that mark because I was never seen studying for the exams at all and the highest mark the Professor had given to any student ever since he started lecturing at University was a 55%. This is what the *anointing within* can do for you if you are sensitive enough to depend or rely more on it than on your brains.

However, the *anointing within* operates on different laws from the anointing upon. They work on totally separate laws. The anointing within you is for yourself while the anointing UPON is for others. The *anointing upon* produces or demonstrates *power* but the anointing within demonstrates *character*. When the *anointing within* is strong in a person, that person will have a strong *Christ like character* but when the anointing is strong upon a person then he would have *great demonstration of the works* of the Holy Spirit because Jesus said in Acts 1:8 *when the Holy Spirit is come upon you, you shall receive power*. The greater truth is that the *anointing upon demonstrates the mighty works of God* but the anointing within demonstrates *the role of God in our lives* and produces fruits of love, joy, peace, patience, kindness, goodness, faithfulness, gentleness, and self-control as illustrated in illustrated in (Galatians 5:22-23). The *anointing within* deals with *exousia* while the *anointing upon* deals with *dunamis*. *Exousia* is delegated authority and power. *Dunamis* refers to the demonstration of the power of the Holy Spirit. That is more frequently used of the *anointing upon*. *Exousia* means the authority of the believer that God has given *and* is always used of the *anointing within*.

This explains why some believers have faltered in their walk with God because they failed to strike a balance between the *anointing upon* and *anointing within* them. For example, some ministers have had a strong *anointing upon* them which initially came through God's grace in which He bestowed spiritual gifts through His own choice (Romans 11:2), but these individuals have had failures, with some falling from ministry and never fully recovering. The question is: How possible is it that such anointed people could fall: How does a tragedy like this happen? The reason a spiritual collapse takes place is because the inward anointing which comprises of biblical morals, holy character, humility, and other spiritual attributes was deficient in that person's life. The inward anointing was not valued or developed, so, such an individual could not support the weight of the anointing of God that is able to come upon a person. We see this clearly in the life of Samson. What a mighty anointing that he had that would come upon him! The nation of Israel had never seen anything like it before. But we all know the unfortunate outcome of his life. It's how we finish that's important, not necessarily how we start out. It is up to us to train ourselves to be diligent and instantly obedient to following the inward anointing. By doing so we will partake of the fruits of obedience which God richly brings forth.

It is a typical scenario in the body of Christ that sometimes a person who has the *anointing upon* knows how to move in that anointing but he does not know how to move with the *anointing within*. As a consequence a person can have a very strong gift of the Spirit operating but his character would be lacking. The anointing within flows forth in Christ like character. And when you put on the anointing within you become more like Christ. Therefore, it is not only important to tap on the *anointing upon*, but you have to deal personally with your character and your mind since the converts are going to receive from your spirit also, whether they see or not depends on your personal life. If a minister who has developed the *anointing within* has a strong Christian character manifested in patience, kind, long-suffering and so forth and all the nine fruits of the Holy Spirit are with him, you could even say that is the character of Christ. But the person has not learned to step in the *anointing upon*. So, he has only got half a point in the area of the *anointing upon*. Therefore, he takes a long time to get a convert. If we are going to win the whole world by the *anointing within* until Christ comes, you will never be able to reach the whole world. Why? It is because the *anointing within* is not enough. That is why Jesus Christ tells His disciples not to ever leave Jerusalem until the *anointing upon* has come. All you need is one miracle and three thousand people will come to know the Lord. In these last days, we need to learn to operate in both dimensions of anointing in order to render an unprecedented avalanche of billions of souls across the globe into the Kingdom.

However, even though these are two different aspects in the realm of the anointing, it must be expressly understood that the *anointing within* and the *anointing upon* do not work in isolation. Instead, there is an intricate connection between the two in terms of the nature of their operation. The greater truth is that the *anointing within* you is what supports the potential anointing that can rest upon you. Therefore, there is a dimension whereby an individual integrates an optimum combination of both realms of the anointing to produce excellent results of power, miracles, healings, and prosperity. In that realm, when one ministers to people, what flows out of him is an optimum combination of the *anointing upon* and *anointing within*. Expressly, when the *anointing upon* is accompanied or mingled with the *anointing within*, it produces edification, gratification and success. The *anointing upon* draws people and produces demonstration of the works of the Holy Spirit while the *anointing within* will affect their character.

It is therefore evident that whenever you want to successfully minister in the Holy Spirit, you have to develop both the *anointing within* and learn to tap on the *anointing upon*. When the *anointing within* your character increases and your *anointing upon* also, then you minister in *quality and quantity*. Therefore, if you flow in the oil of the spirit in the *anointing upon*, the anointing upon is still guided by the *anointing within*. Everything that you flow in the *anointing upon*, your *anointing within* will guide you. We do not move out from operating by the *anointing within*. For example, to be a prophet you will have to have two revelation gifts and the gift of prophecy. Your revelation gifts could operate by visions. So you constantly see visions and you foretell what God has given to you. While you are moving in visions, whatever vision you see needs to be guided and confirmed by the *anointing within* the anointing within will guide us in moving in the *anointing upon*. The *anointing within* guards the *anointing upon*. So the *anointing within* is important. It is the key to guidance to operate the *anointing upon*. So the *anointing upon* and the *anointing within* works together. And by God's grace we can learn to operate both of them.

THE IMPACT OF THE ANOINTING UPON HUMAN VESELS

A Practical Demonstration Of What The Anointing Can Do In You

It must be expressly understood that the anointing is an impartation of God's ability. Therefore, when it comes, there must be a corresponding change and an undeniably notable difference in the life of a vessel. The greater truth is that when the anointing comes upon a vessel, God's ability is so much that the person changes both in character, behaviour and personality. There are instantaneous, drastic, significant and clear cut changes that comes with the anointing upon a vessel. However, a person may not permanently change or differ in personality although in most cases such changes affect the recipient's personality, behaviour, character, conduct, perception, reasoning capacity, mentality and above all else, vision. In other words, a person who receives the anointing upon acquires the exact spiritual faculties of God to operate like God on earth. It is like God acting through a man. It is like God has gotten hold of the spirit of a man and begins to operate His faculties through him. It is like God operating through a man and doing only those things which man cannot do but which God can do. But the truth of the matter is that there must be a change when the anointing comes.

Deeper Revelations Of The anonting

The act of having received an *anointing upon* is unequivocally evident in a human body such that it cannot be concealed or hidden. The anointing is such a tangible and visible spiritual substance that its manifestation is undeniably real even to the natural senses. In the natural realm, a man cannot jump into a pool of water and come out dry. By the same token, you cannot say that you have received an anointing from God and not be able to show it or affect the people around you. Therefore, no one can claim to be anointed or moving in the anointing when there is no tangible evidence to back up his claim. Whenever the anointing is in operation, the dead are raised, the crippled made to walk, blind eyes opened and incurable sicknesses healed instantaneously. There is no such a thing called a *gradual healing in the realm of the anointing.*The nature of the ingredient of the anointing is such that it affects something. It overwhelmingly impacts your sphere of influence or contact once it has been released upon a human vessel. The anointing cannot be kept a secret; instead, there will be a definite, evident, tangible and visible change when it comes upon you. It is said that when Smith Wigglesworth preached, sometimes when he started out, he just wouldn't make sense because he was not educated. He would stumble around but then the Spirit of God would come on him. The anointing would startle the congregation because they could literally see it in action. His countenance would change, and the words would just flow out of his mouth. It looked like he had *turned into another man.*

Benny Hinn, one of the World's Heavy Weight Generals, who are striding at the frontline in the global demonstration of the anointing, concurs with this revelation and asserts that often times a person called to a ministry involving speaking before an audience literally feels an anointing descend upon them as they begin to minister, and they may even be a changed person full of boldness and authority while under the influence of that anointing if normally they are shy and quiet. Then after two or three hours after ministering, the anointing may lift. The same example could hold true of those anointed to prophesy. Normally they may be reserved and quiet, but when the anointing comes on them for ministry, they are a completely different person until the anointing lifts after they have finished ministering. People called to the healing ministry, while under the influence of the anointing for ministry, may feel literal heat, electricity and power coming out of their hands, or may operate in words of knowledge, and be unusually bold.

In view of the above, it is therefore unequivocally evident that the anointing brings about a tangible change upon those vessels it rests upon. However, it is worth noting that the change depends on the measure we receive, the manner in which we receive it, our level of expectancy to receive it and our attitude when we receive it. Sometimes it is a lesser measure and sometimes it is a greater measure of the anointing we receive but whether it is greater or lesser but the bottom line is that change would have been effected. The anointing effects a change in you so that we could say you are changed to another person. This is because something different shows up after the anointing came. Whether it is of a greater or lesser difference, there must be something. The behaviour manifested by the bible's legends such as Samson, Elijah, Saul and David's mighty men gives a clear pictorial representation of the intensity and gravity of the impact of the anointing upon a human vessel. Therefore the following experiences or cases of encounter in the anointing will help you understand what it means to receive or operate in the dimension of the anointing. There are key lessons that we can learn from the Bible legends based on their experience in the anointing.

CASES OF SPIRITUAL ENCOUNTERS AND EXPERIENCES THAT RESULTS FROM THE IMPACT OF THE ANOINTING

THE CASE OF SAUL: THE OPERATION OF "SAULIC" (KINGLY ANOINTING)

To illustrate the impact of the anointing upon a human vessel, let's start by examining the life of Saul after the anointing came upon his life. To give you a background of the story, under normal circumstances, Saul was just a timid guy who had an inferiority complex prior to him receiving the anointing. Just like a multitude of believers across the globe, he was so caught up in his past circumstances such that the consciousness of his social upbringing and status clouded his vision to believe God for greater things. In spite of his favourable physical stature as a tall and well-built man, he felt as inferior as a tiny little kitten. How do I know this? It's because when he met Samuel and Samuel said to him, *"God has chosen you,"* the first thing Saul said is, *"Who am I? Who is my father's house? I come from the smallest family of the smallest tribe."* In other words, Saul did not want to be in the limelight but when the Spirit of God came on him, his story changed and he became a different person. Just like Saul, many people inadvertently believe that because of their poor background and social upbringing, they cannot go far with God because their past has a way of catching up with them but when the anointing comes upon them, it is a different story. The anointing changes your past, re-writes your history and present a different story to what people perceived you to be. In I Samuel 10:1, the Bible records that,

> *Samuel took a flask of oil and poured it on his head, and kissed him and said, You shall come to the hill of God where the Philistine garrison is. And it will happen, when you have come there to the city that you will see a group of prophets coming down from the high place with a stringed instrument, a tambourine, a flute, and a harp before them; and they will be prophesying. Then the Spirit of the Lord will come upon you, and you will prophesy with them and* be **turned into another man.**

There is something striking about Saul's experience in the anointing. The Bible says after the anointing came upon him, he was *turned into another man*. But what does it mean, to be *"turned into another man"*? What did he become like? Does it mean that he assumed the form of another man? Does it mean that his physical appearance or countenance changed to be like his somebody else? Definitely not. The greater truth is that when the bible talks about being, **"turned into another man,**

> *It describes more of a condition of a drastic change in character, personality and behaviour than just physical form or appearance.* It means that *there is a possibility of taking a different personality, different thought pattern, different behaviour, different emotions as if a new personality is added to you.*

Allegorically speaking, when the Holy Spirit comes upon you, you are *turned into another man in the sense that the anointing gets hold of all your natural faculties and changes your character in such a way that you can even act, speak, preach like a completely different person.* Something drastic must have taken place. In other words, Saul was never the same person after the anointing came. The anointing has the power to turn you into a different person. That is why when you move and operate under an anointing, you feel like you are a different personality altogether. I have observed in my experience in the anointing, that there are times when the anointing comes upon me, that I start moving and operating in super intelligence, accuracy of speech and my articulation abilities and degree of eloquence advances to such an extent that even my natural assent, command of language and tone changes. People whom I work with especially those who usually see me during the ordinary course of life at times get the shock of their life when they see me on stage operating under the anointing because they always exclaim that I am *a different man* than what they are used to see.

A quintessential example is Kathryn Kuhlman, who described her experience under an anointing as being *out of the body experience*. She says she feels like she is just outside and somebody else was speaking through her when the anointing is operating. That is a very high level of anointing of God. The anointing is like another part of a personality taking you over so that literally when you yield to it, you could be like a different person. Now, the anointing does not force us but we have to yield to it. If you really yield to that anointing, you are like a different person. What happened in the yielded stage was his first experience. Saul yielded to it and he was a different person.

In view of the above, that means you could be the lowliest man in terms of how people perceive you in the society, you could be from a poor family or background, you could be having an inferiority complex, despised, dejected, not respected or counted for nothing in the world but when the anointing comes upon you, there is a sudden turnaround of situations and circumstances from a zero to a hero, from ashes to beauty, from nobody to somebody and from a servant to a master. This is what the anointing is capable of doing when it comes upon a vessel. I have seen that the majority of the people who have shaken this world by God's power and anointing are those who grew up shy, dejected, alienated and taken for granted but when the anointing rested upon them their story changed.

THE CASE OF SAMSON: THE OPERATION OF "SAM SONIC" (LIONIC ANOINTING)

Samson is one of the Bible legends who moved in the anointing like a soldier sent out for a conquest. Contrary to how the people of the world has portrayed him, under normal circumstances, Samson was just a skinny, ordinary man, but when the anointing came upon him, it gave him super-human strength to do the impossible, things which could not be performed by man in his reasonable or ordinary capacity. Philosophically speaking, he became a *superman*. He accomplished great victories over the bear, the lion, the foxes, and the Philistines just by the anointing and ability given by God. This implies that you could be the skinniest tiny little lady in the world but when the Samsonic anointing comes on you, you could lift an elephant with just the tip of your small finger. You could be the most fearful, timid and confused person in your family but when the anointing comes upon you, you can challenge whatever powers whether spiritual or physical.

Deeper Revelations Of The anonting

Samson was a powerful man under the anointing but when the anointing was not there, he was easily influenced, easily falling for women because he did not know how to rein his personality and subject it to his anointing.

His achievements through the anointing were so remarkable such that his behaviour and character was even metamorphosed. He was so infused and mingled with the anointing such that he lived in the anointing, by the anointing and for the anointing. He became who he was *by reason of the anointing*. The Bible says in the absence of the anointing, Samson was nothing but a powerless freak but when the anointing came upon him, he moved in power and tremendously impacted lives. This implies that his identity was in the anointing since without the anointing he was nothing. This is the extent of the dimension and realm of the anointing which Samson taped into. The anointing is what defines who you are. Your true identity is in the anointing. Therefore, the essence of humanity is found in the anointing because the anointing is what defines you. In the realm of the spirit people are known by the measure of the anointing upon their lives. As much as in the natural realm people are known by their academic credentials, in the spirit dimension our credential is the anointing. Our positions of influence and power are determined by how much anointing we have. Therefore, the greater the anointing, the higher the authority and influence in the supernatural and the opposite is true.

Moreover, the size of a blessing any man can receive from God is always directly proportional to the size of his anointing. This is because the anointing is a river through which our blessings flow from the throne room to be imparted on us. If the river of the anointing is not there then there is no ways our blessings could flow from the spirit realm into the physical realm. Every spiritual blessing requires an anointing for it to flow and transmute itself into a tangible and visible form in the physical realm. In the same way cars do not travel without petrol, blessings are not released in the absence of an anointing because the anointing is a lubricant that facilitates the shift movement of substances between the realm of the spirit and the natural. Prayers, faith, worship is presented to God through the anointing and on the other hand answers, blessings and breakthroughs are released from heaven through the anointing hence, the anointing is what synchronises, harmonises or brings the two realms of existence together. This explains the reasons why some people's blessings have been delayed because they have not earnestly sought after the precious ingredient of the anointing.

Frequency Revelator

THE CASE OF ELIJAH: THE OPERATION OF "THE PROPHETIC ANOINTING"

Elijah is one of the Bible legends who functioned mightily in the realm of *territorial anointing*. He learnt how to tap into the realm of the anointing to accomplish tasks in both the supernatural and the natural realms. When the anointing came upon Elijah, he too experienced supernatural strength just like Samson but the *Elijahic anointing* is unique as compared to the *Samsonic anointing*. In the case of Elijah, not only did the anointing give him supernatural strength to have victories over things in the natural but it also gave him the ability to rule in the supernatural to such an extent that he opened and closed the heavens at his own prerogative. Imagine Elijah taking the keys and locking the heavens and angels are just looking at him and could not even question him. Imagine some angels did not even have they keys of heaven but Elijah had them. He even had a spare key into God's throne room. That was a realm beyond the authority of angels. That is why God caught him up and translated him to heaven and did not allow him to see decay because he operated under a heavy anointing and lived above the realm of angels. While still on earth, Elijah knew heaven like the back of his hand and lived there more than he did in the natural. His secret was in the anointing.

In I Kings 18, after the land had gone for three and a half years without rain, because Elijah had closed the heavens, he met the King Ahab and declared,

"I hear the sound of the abundance of rain"

He then told King Ahab to rush back to Jezreel because rain was coming. King Ahab started riding in his chariot but under the anointing, Elijah ran faster than King Ahab's chariot. How can a man run faster than the fastest of all animals, the best fed horse in the country? This was an *overtaking anointing* that came upon him. It was God's supernatural ability which caused him to do all these tasks beyond human and physical capabilities. This is what the anointing does when it comes upon a yielded vessel. Just like Elijah, who opened and closed heavens at his own prerogative, with the anointing, you could determine the destiny of nations, impact the world for Christ and invade new territories for the kingdom. The anointing is what gives you authority over subjects both in the natural and spirit realm. You can reign over territories just like Smith Wigglesworth who would not allow anybody in his neighbourhood to die without his permission. In other words he became a chief decision maker concerning who should die and who should not and heaven endorsed that decision hence, all forces of divinity were compelled to work on his behalf as heavens' attention was directed towards him.

THE CASE OF ELISHA THE OPERATION OF "THE DOUBLE PORTION ANOINTING"

Elisha was well known for functioning in the greater depths of the realm of the miraculous. He performed so many miracles, signs and wonders recorded in the bible through the double portion anointing he had received from Elijah. Before that, he was just an ordinary servant who followed and served Elijah wherever he went but when he finally got the double portion anointing, his case changed. Immediately, he confronted the river Jordan and demonstrated the power of God by dividing its waters. This is the impact of the *transition anointing*. Just like Elisha whom upon receiving the double portion anointing instantly demonstrated the power of God, immediately after receiving the anointing, all the ways, doors and opportunities in your life are opened and the results of success are immediate and instantaneous. This implies that you don't have to wait long for your case or situation to change. Elisha's status also changed instantaneously. He became the leader of the prophets in a flip of a moment. With the anointing, you don't need to wait for ten years for your boss to resign at work for you to get a promotion. Just because of the anointing upon your life, your progress in terms of promotion must be immediate and instantaneous.

Regardless of your profile, status, position, level of education, background, social affiliation or how people perceive you in life, the anointing can change your status and position from a domestic worker like Elisha to a Director of School of prophets. The anointing had so permeated the core of his being such that even four hundred years after his death, his bones still retained the anointing. When certain men were burying a dead man long after Elisha had departed, the moment the dead man came into contact with the bones of Elisha, he rose from the dead. Wow! This is remarkable. This is the greatest of all miracles not performed by Elisha only but recorded in the whole bible. Imagine the bones raising a man from the dead! So many believers in our generation cannot not even heal the sick or let alone raise the dead but Elisha whom without a hand or a mouth but just a pile of bones raised a man from the dead. Wow! This shows the long lasting impact that the anointing can have on a human being. Bones are a symbol of dryness or a dry situation. The bones of Elisha were exposed and did not even have any flesh but because of the anointing they performed wonders. Just like the dry bones, you might be in a desert of lack, in a place of dryness in your finances, ministry or family, you might be have been exposed, humiliated, busted and embarrassed in life but when the anointing rests upon your life, miracles of uncommon favour, unlimited financial breakthrough, signs and wonders will flow to you from every side.

THE CASE OF DAVID AND HIS MIGHTY MEN:

THE OPERATION OF "DAVIDIC" (WARRING ANOINTING)

The Bible records that during the time of war, one of David's mightymen fought to such an extent that *his hand cleaved to the sword.* In other words, his sword and his hand were like one and the same thing. This implies that in the natural realm, one could not differentiate clearly whether his hand was the sword or the sword was his hand. He fought so hard and so long that his hand cleaved to the sword. Wow! This was such a spectacular display of the anointing. That is what happens when the anointing changes your personality. It is therefore evident that David's special ability as a mighty soldier and warrior came from the anointing upon his life (2 Samuel 22:33-35). It was not a natural ability but it was a supernatural impartation that trained his hands for war and his arms to bend a bow of bronze. Have you ever wondered why God said *David is a man after my own heart?* What exactly is it that David did which granted him such an honour and favour? Is it because he was the greatest warrior? Definitely not. This is because David functioned or moved well in the anointing more than any other person in the history of the bible. He knew how to make use of the anointing in such a way that gained him favour with God. He progressively exercised his anointing over the lion, the bear even long before he became a king and at each stage, God promoted him because he knew how to effectively utilise the precious commodity of heaven, which is the anointing.

David and his men were warriors and conquers but the Bible says *we are more than the conquerors.* This implies that we can tap into and exceed or surpass this dimension of the *warring anointing* which David and his men tapped into in the realm of *spiritual warfare* and *territorial governance.* You might have been side-lined by people for long like David, you might have stayed in the cave of your suffering, lack, limitation in progress for a long time, you might have lived a life of being hunted by enemies, left, right and centre like David. You might have been given a stigma or called by names or labelled a thief, prostitute, nonentity, or associated with lowlife, low class, gone through several phases of failure and defeat in life and counted for nothing but when the anointing comes upon you, it will open doors and bring opportunities for success, promotion and you will rise to the highest ranks in life than you have never imagined. It is all possible through the anointing. The anointing breeds favour, opportunities and a strong magnetic force or power to attract all good things to you.

Despite your background and social status, with the anointing, you can marry the most beautiful lady in the world, drive the most expensive car in the country, live in the best places in the town, occupy the best seat in society, reach the highest rank at work or in business, command the highest position of respect and honour in the society. It is all possible through the anointing. The anointing will bring fame, favour and honour, charisma, dignity, make you a role model and cause people who never took notice of you to celebrate you. As a matter of fact, there are two things that makes one to be a celebrity in this world, that is money and the anointing but the latter by far exceeds any monetary value of property in this world because money is the currency of this world but the anointing is the currency of heaven.

THE CASE OF PETER: THE OPERATION OF "PETERSIC" (LEADERSHIP ANOINTING)

Peter is one of the apostles who had quite a number of prominent faults and heightened weaknesses, yet he is the one who moved and tapped into greater dimensions of the anointing more than other apostles in his generation. At one point in time, he was so scared for his life that He denied Jesus three times and even after the resurrection and ascension of Jesus, fear still gripped him even though he was the leader of the apostles such that he mobilised all the disciples into the upper room in fear of persecution. The upper room was located in the highest, isolated and extremely quiet part of the building where no one would even bother to go there. But when the anointing came upon him, he boldly declared the word of God and confronted the atheism of the rulers and governors with God's power. The anointing is such that it actually has the potential to change you if you keep flowing in it long enough. It is like a habit which is formed if you keep repeating the action for a long time. If you keep yielding to a certain characteristic of the anointing, it can become a part of your life and change and transform you. You begin to develop an understanding why people have failings and faults and begin to teach the Word as an antidote and solution to their problems.

You might have a multitudes of weaknesses and faults like Peter and have people judge you, criticise or despise you but when the anointing comes upon your life, you will be catapulted from the upper room of your fear, weakness and limitations to the greatest heights of nations of the world and from the upper room of your lack to millions of wealth. In another occasion, the anointing had soaked through his life such that his shadow became a point of contact for healing the nations. One major characteristic feature of a shadow is just its can only be seen or visible when there is light because it is the refection of your body by light; if it's cloudy, rainy or dark, it cannot be seen. But Peter's shadow operated on a different principle when the anointing came upon him, whether it was dark or raining or cloudy, his shadow was seen falling on the sick and performing miracles. You might not be on the lime light right now, you might be enduring the darkest moments of your life, you might have been thrown into the life's deep end but when the anointing comes upon you, you can operate like a shadow whether it is dark or what. At one point, Peter moved in greater depths of the anointing such that as he was preaching the Holy Ghost fell upon all those who heard his voice. This is a greater realm of anointing which he tapped into, an *overflow anointing*. All these accomplishments came as a result of the anointing.

THE CASE OF PAUL & THE APOSTLES: THE OPERATION OF "APOSTOLIC ANOINTING"

The Bible puts on record that after the ascension of Jesus into heaven, the apostles were gathered together in the upper room in timidity and fear of death and persecution but when the Holy Ghost came upon them at Pentecost and rubbed the anointing on them, they became a different breed of people shaking the world with the power of the gospel. The Bible says onlookers even wondered and exclaimed *"Are these man not Galileans,"* because of the level of boldness they displayed under the anointing. You could be a soft-spoken lady but when the anointing comes upon you, you could preach like a machine gun. People do not understand the impact the anointing can have on your personality. You could be different when the anointing is upon you. It could turn you into another man or another woman. The likes of Apostle Paul was so anointed that he wrote a third of the bible. It takes a great deal of anointing to write the bible. He had a *revelational anointing*. The greater depths of the writing anointing upon him launched him into the realm of revelation. The gospel he preached was not taught by any man but received by revelation. This is a *revelation anointing* at work.

You might not have a theological background or not gone to a Bible school but when the *revelation anointing* comes, it can food your spirit with revelations of God's word such that even the best bible scholars will wonder if they are using the same bible as you do or you got yours directly from heaven. The anointing that came upon Paul was so strong such that immediately after getting born again he preached the gospel of the Lord Jesus Christ and moved in power. Under normal circumstances, it takes time for people after getting born again to preach, let alone move in the anointing but in the case of Paul, it was a different story. Many people usually go through some phases of ministry from the time they get born again up to when they finally get an opportunity to preach, but Paul preached immediately after getting born again because of the higher dimension of the anointing that had rested upon him. With the anointing, you can be catapulted to higher realms of glory straight after salvation. It is not necessary to stay ten years in church before you could demonstrate the power of God. Just one week is enough to learn how to tap in the realm of the anointing because things move so fast in the realm of the spirit. Paul had so many weaknesses, his foundation was faulty, he was a murderer, he had the blood of saints in his hands. Some disciples were even scared of him even after he was born again, but despite all these negativities of life when the anointing rested upon him, he became the number one apostle in his generation. You can have the worst history of being a thief, murderer, prostitute or robber but when the anointing rests upon you, you could shake the whole world with God's power just like what Apostle Paul did. The secret is in the *anointing*.

THE CASE OF STEPHEN: THE OPERATION OF "STEPHANIC" (EXPLOSIVE ANOINTING)

The Bible says in Acts 6:5-8 that Stephen was so highly anointed such that God performed so many miracles, signs and wonders by his hand. Even up to the point of death, the anointing was so strong upon Stephen such that even when they were stoning him, he was just busy watching a movie going on in heaven. He saw heavens opening and God sitting on throne and Jesus at His right hand. This is remarkable! Can you imagine as they were killing him, he was busy making an announcement, reporting what's going on in Heaven! That can only be possible under the anointing. Even at death, with the anointing, the pangs of death are disabled. In actual fact, one does not die under the anointing but he sleeps. Stephen slept. There was no pain involved. You can be on the verge of death, you can be going through the valley of the shadow of death as David confessed, with a multitude of enemies, left, right and centre but when the anointing comes upon you, a thousand shall fall on your side and ten thousand on your left hand. Why are they falling? Because of the anointing.

The anointing is the Spirit of God, with due respect to Him, *possessing you."* His personality is so powerful that He could possess you until you become an extension of His being. Stephen was described as being full of wisdom in Acts 6:5 whereas Jesus was described as coming in the power of the Spirit in Luke 4: 14. That means that the anointing is actually the Spirit possessing us. Think about that – it is powerful. The anointing is not just a sword He gives you and then you go and fight. No, it's the Spirit all over you, and possessing you. You are carried by the flow of the Spirit. Just flow along with the Spirit of God . Just be carried by the tidal waves of the Spirit of God. Just go along with that. People might hate you or be jealous of your talents, gifting or achievements to the extent of wrongly accusing you or drag your name in the mud or tarnish your good reputation like Stephen but with the anointing they cannot resist the wisdom of the Spirit operating in your life

THE CASE OF JESUS: THE OPERATION OF "MESSIAHIC ANOINTING"

Some people think that just because Jesus was the son of God, he did not feel any pain or impact of any challenge whenever he encountered opposition. This is heresy. The Bible says in Philippians 2:7 that He was made in the likeness of a sinful man and striped of all the Glory he had. He became flesh and dwelt amongst man. This implies that he too was subject to the limitations of humanity. He faced the cross as a man, he faced death and was crucified as a man but because of the measureless anointing that was upon him, he endured through all trials and tribulation and came out victorious. He came out of the cross with a testimony, he triumphed over sin and death and all satanic powers, sickness could not touch him, he prevailed in all situations and ultimately obtained the crown of life and received greater glory. Today, the whole universe is enjoying the fruits of His anointing. When you have the anointing on your life and you learn to flow with it like Jesus, you have the potential to become a totally different person. The anointing need not change your personality but it can. You could flow into it so much so that the anointing becomes your nature and you become part of the anointing.

Deeper Revelations Of The anonting

You might be going through the worst trails and facing the greatest challenges and situations which you think no one has ever faced in this life, but with the anointing upon you, you will wear a smile when no one is making a joke, you will be lifted, you will leave a legacy, you will be a hero in your generation, you will make a long life impact, you will lay an unshakable and unwavering foundation for the future generations to come, you will set a pace or trend and rise above all situations, you will leave a track record of honour, you will create and re-write your own history, you will break your own record, you will conquer all situations and come out with an Msc Degree (Masters in situations and circumstances). This can only be possible through the anointing.

CHAPTER FOUR

DEVINE QUALIFICATIONS AND CREDENTIALS FOR OPERATING IN THE REALM OF THE ANOINTING

How To Attract, Trigger And Provoke The Flow of The Anointing Upon Your Life

It must be fully understood that the anointing is the supernatural ability of God imparted upon human beings. It is the most special, delicate and elegant treasure given to man by God. It is such a precious spiritual substance or heavenly commodity whose value is like the currency that regulates the economy of heaven. It is so sacred, pure, precious, flamboyant, glamorous, superlative and magnificent more than the value of any product or currency in the whole universe. It is more glamorous and glittering than the value of gold, silver and diamonds or the most expensive and precious stones of the universe.

However, it must be expressly understood that in order to operate and function is such a powerful heavenly grace, the anointing must be tapped, stirred and provoked into manifestation. This is because the anointing flows out like a river in food right from the centre of God's throne and cascades down to filter into every sphere of humanity on earth. In essence, there is a river whose waters are as clear as crystal that originates from the centre of the throne room and spreads and flows down to the earth and this river carries *the anointing*. Under ordinary circumstances, the anointing does not just flow automatically upon the masses and that is why there is no such a thing called an *automatic anointing*. Instead, the anointing has to be stirred, provoked, activated in order to flow or operate just like the pool of Bethsaida had to be stirred by an angel to bring forth the healing virtue (John 5:1-16). In the same way the angel had to stir the waters of the pool of Bethsaida so that anybody who jumped in first received his healing, connecting to this river is the key or breakthrough into the realm of *the anointing*. The following are divergent ways through which the anointing could be triggered or provoked into manifestation.

The ability to withstand and pass tests and trials

Despite the fact that in the New Testament dispensation every believer has total and unrestricted access to all heavenly blessings of which the anointing is a part, it is of paramount significance to unveil the divine truth that by virtue of its valuable, delicate and elegant nature, God does not give the anointing that easily. One of the ways through which one qualifies to have the anointing finally resting on him in a greater measure is the ability to pass diverse tests and trials. That is why Abraham was tested before God could release Isaac. There are a series of tests and trails which one has to go through before the anointing could rests upon a vessel. Tests and trials are divine qualifications and credentials for receiving the anointing. In other words, one has to qualify or graduate for the anointing to come just like a student passes the tests to qualify for graduation. That is why Paul says we must through many tribulations enter the kingdom. The phrase *enter the kingdom'* speaks of manifesting the anointing or power of God.

However, it is a typical scenario in the Christian faith that many people cry out for the anointing but then fail to pass God's tests hence it never rests upon them. On the other extreme, many people ask God to anoint them to prosper but they have never proven themselves in every test in their lives and hence they block God's blessings. Metaphorically speaking, as the heat intensifies, many jump out of the frying pan hence they never get the chance to be fried, cooked and roasted by the fire. Moreover, some people are zealous to do exploits and demonstrate the power of God through miracles, signs and wonders but they never pass the tests which come alongside the administration of that grace hence, the anointing never manifest in their lives. Others abort the vision of God while still at conception stage hence, they never get to the level where they qualify to graduate to the next level of the *anointing*. In view of the above, it must be understood that even if one might have a call of God upon his life, that does not guarantee that the anointing will automatically rests upon him until he passes the test. In other words, the anointing is not automatically given to anyone but its release is based on passing tests and trials and these differ according to the level of our callings. Figuratively speaking, not every woman can carry a child; a malnutritioned woman will not be able to carry the weight of the child in the womb. By the same token, a man who has not been qualified through trials will be able to carry the greater weight of the anointing. While in some cases tests and trials might be hurting and painful to the flesh, they cause such a tremendous effect on the spirit man such that it is able to bear a greater weight of glory. That is why Paul says *our current afflictions are just but for a moment and are not worthy compared to the greater weight of glory which shall rest upon us*. However, it must be understood expressly that in the context of this revelation, trials and tribulations do not refer to people suffering due to ignorance, sickness or demonic oppression but it refers to divine tests which are orchestrated in the realm of the spirit and are within the framework of God's will and purpose.

A significant degree of consecration manifested or exhibited by a vessel

It is worth mentioning that with regard to matters of the supernatural, there are absolutely no shortcuts to operating in the anointing of God and never will be. A significant level of consecration is one of the divine catalysts and prerequisites to provoking the perennial flow of the anointing of God in ones' life. The anointing that God puts on His servants is such a precious commodity that God expects a significantly high degree of consecration from His vessels before He could invest it upon them. In the same way the banker demands collateral or asurity before he could release humongous funds, the anointing is an investment of God's power in humanity hence, God demands consecration before that investment could be made. Consecration implies living a life that is uncompromisingly holy, sacred and totally set apart from the world. In a practical sense, consecration speaks of a total, unreserved dependence and devotion to meditation, studying and assimilation of God's word, deep fellowship with the Holy spirit, practice of God's presence as well as undertaking key spiritual exercises such as prayer and fasting on a regular basis as well as a conscientious or diligent application of spiritual laws and principles of the kingdom.

To illustrate the gravity of the spiritual laws and principles governing the operation of the anointing in Leviticus 8:33-35, Aaron was instructed that the anointing he received was so holy that he could not leave the tabernacle for seven days or else he will die. In a related incident in Leviticus 10:6, when a sad event involving the death of his family members happened, Eli was not even allowed to cry or let alone bury the dead. In Exodus 19:10, the Lord said unto Moses, *Go unto the people, and sanctify them today and tomorrow, and let them wash their clothes for on the third day I will come*. In other words, it took a significant level of consecration for the glory of God to show up. This is the essence of consecration. It actually shows how sacred the anointing is. While in the New Testament dispensation we have unreserved and unrestricted access to the anointing and the glory, however the principle of consecration still stands. While God changes in line with His times and seasons, His nature, character as well as divine methodological operations, does not change. Therefore, in order to move into greater depths of the anointing, one would have to consecrate himself by being set apart from the distractive elements of this world. The anointing was strictly given for sanctification. Sanctification infers purification, separated for service or holiness. The Bible records in Leviticus 8:12 that *Moses poured the anointing oil upon Aaron's head, and anointed him, to sanctify him.* The anointing was not just for a person, but for places and things separated unto God. There was an anointing on the Ark of the Covenant which prevented just anyone from touching it.

And you shall take the anointing oil, and anoint the tabernacle, and all that is therein, and shalt hallow it, and all the vessels thereof: and it shall be holy (Exodus 40:9).

The greater truth is that the level of the anointing will vary according to the believer's preparedness. Sometimes, Christians are more prepared than at other times. Sometimes they may be able to spend time waiting on God more than other times. It is important to spend time in fellowship and intimacy with God in order to build up a preparedness to move when the Spirit moves. By being prepared, Christians are more able to tap into the full measure of the anointing upon their life. There is a price to pay in anointed ministry, such as waiting upon the Lord, praying, fasting, studying the Word and seeking the mind of the Spirit. There are sacrifices that have to be made in order to walk in God's fullness. Preparedness affects the anointing of God upon an individual's life. The reality is that many ministers are not able to launch into greater depths of the anointing because they do not spend time in the presence of God. In the same way a baby is not given birth within one month of pregnancy, the anointing is also not released by just piping and part timing is God's presence for few seconds. It takes a significance level of intimacy for conception to take place in the natural realm. By the same token, it takes a significant level of intimacy with the Holy Spirit for the anointing to be given birth to in the spirit. Therefore, when God places a call upon a person, He expects total submission. This almost always means turning off the voice of the flesh. Jesus said that He sanctified Himself for the purpose of anointed ministry (John 17). In other words, He consecrated Himself because He had such a high mission for the sheep hence.

A High level of spiritual sacrifice exhibited by the vessel

It is a divine truth that the anointing requires a spiritual sacrifice to be offered by the vessel. Before the anointing could rests on vessels, there is a sacrificial price that has to be paid. However, too many people look at the wrong side of anointing. They see the anointing seem so easy on some ministers' lives. They can quote many stories of men of God whose characters and lives were not up to the mark, how they fell and disgraced the name of Christ. What they don't realise is that these men initially made sacrifices in the spirit but after the anointing came, they became complacent and slowly lost the anointing. The gifts and calling of God are given without repentance but the anointing to function in these gifts and calling of God can be taken away. Although there is a grace period for such fallen ministers to repent and change, the grace period is not forever. So, remember this whenever you hear stories of fallen ministers, don't think that the anointing is cheap. It is not cheap. It is very expensive and priceless. For example, when Elisha said, *"I want a double portion of the spirit in you,"* Elijah said, *"You have asked a hard thing."* By this he meant that there is a price that you pay to qualify to access greater, deeper and high measures of the anointing. Once you paid the price and you move into it, you've got to maintain your consecration before God to hit on to higher heights. But there is a breakthrough point that you move into.

Some times when we see great men of God like Benny Hinn or Pastor Chris, who move in greater dimensions of the anointing of God, we tend to say, *"Well, it's by the grace of God that they have it,"* and we think that there is no price involved. Kathryn Kuhlman concurs that there is a price you pay. The greater truth is that every man or woman of God who have ever operated the anointing have paid a price somewhere in their lives before the anointing started operating. However, it happens that later some people have lost the anointing in their lives because they stopped paying the price hence their character and their ministry are no longer in harmony with the ministry. In other words, they have learned the art of moving into the anointing but they are no more paying the price. And there is a grace period before the anointing leaves. What we observe of those people that are within the grace period where the anointing is still there but they have stopped paying the price is that God could be so merciful that sometimes the grace period could be quite a number of years.

Deeper Revelations Of The anonting

Degree of consciousness and acknowledgement of the anointing

The extent to which the anointing flows upon one's life is determined by the level of consciousness, awareness or recognition of the anointing. The greater truth is that the spiritual laws that govern angelic operations are almost similar to those that govern the flow of the anointing and one of these spiritual laws is the *principle of acknowledgment of the anointing*. This principle unveils that in order to tap into greater depths of the anointing, one must be aware of the presence of the anointing and acknowledge that he is anointed. Acknowledgment of the anointing means that one has a deep self-conviction that he is surely anointed and has developed a significant level of consciousness to the flow of that anointing.

When you minister the anointing of God, you have to believe that you are anointed. The only way you can believe that you are anointed is to sense that anointing come upon you. I am not talking about exercising faith now. You can believe by faith through the believers' anointing but before you minister the anointing, you have to believe that you are anointed. And when you tangibly know that the anointing is there, it produces confidence in you. And that comes through constant practice. Since every believer has a measure of the anointing, identifying the source of the anointing is key to breaking forth into alarming streams of the anointing. By acknowledging the measure of the anointing, one has, it opens his spirit and accentuates new avenues through which further volumes of the anointing could flow.

In a practical sense, what does it mean to acknowledge the anointing? By acknowledging the anointing, one boldly declares in the spirit that he is anointed and can do all things by the anointing Just like Jesus declared in acknowledgement that *the anointing of the Lord is upon me for He has anointed me to declare the good news to the poor, to heal the broken hearted, to proclaim liberty to the captives and proclaim the acceptable year of the lord.* Encapsulated in Jesus's public declaration in the above mentioned scripture is what we call *an acknowledgement of the anointing*. That is why Jesus moved in greater dimensions of the anointing more than anybody else because He first learnt how to acknowledge, receive and embrace the reality that the anointing was at work in Him and this is an element that is lacking in many believers today because they are so theoretical about the anointing instead of being practical about it. *What effect then does acknowledgement of the anointing have in one's spirit?* The effect is that as you operate in this realm of acknowledgment of the anointing, you open yourself up to the spirit realm hence, there is a positive energy being released into your spirit. Acknowledgement is like a key that opens all doors into the reservoir of the anointing in the supernatural and a tap that provokes a stream flow of further volumes of the anointing to food your spirit.

However, acknowledgment of the anointing does not only refer to acknowledging the anointing that is upon one's life only but also involves acknowledgment of the anointing that is upon a man of God or others. For example, when David finally got a life time window of opportunity to kill Saul, he refused to do so and only cut his robe instead because he acknowledged the anointing of God upon Saul (Samuel 24:5). David said to his men, *"The Lord forbid that I should do this thing to my master, the Lord's anointed, to stretch out my hand against him, seeing he is the anointed of the Lord."* This is a *statement of acknowledgement of the anointing* which I'm talking about. Moreover, it is recorded in I Samuel 26:9 that David said to Abishai, *"Do not destroy him; for who can stretch out his hand against the Lord's anointed and be guiltless?"* This implies that *David recognized the anointing in other people's life and this was a secret and key to his greatness*.

Saul still held his office although he lost his anointing. This is because the gifts and the callings of God are without repentance. He lived out his time even though he lost his anointing. He was called and never lost his call but he lost his anointing but what happen here is that David still recognized the calling and anointing in others. If you learn to recognize the anointing of God in other people, people will recognize it in your life. David could have killed Saul but said, *"No, in spite of his ways, I recognize that God has placed him there. Hence, God is the one to remove him. I won't be the one to remove him."* And he just walked away. He recognized the anointing in others. And everyone whose ministry has grown fast, you will notice that this is one of the keys that they tap on. *What benefits does it have to acknowledge others?* When you promote others, others will promote you. When you try to promote yourself others will pull you down. He that waters others will be watered himself. He that helps others will be helped himself. Do to others what you would want them to do to you. He that runs down others will be run down himself. He that lifts others up, will be lifted up himself. That's how you get into the anointing of God as you help others, as you lift others, and as you recognize the anointing in others, God will unreservedly pour out the rain of His anointing upon you.

Ability to tap into the realm of the anointing from men of

God of the previous generation

There is something critical that this generation has not grasped as yet concerning the anointing. Due to lack of revelation, multitudes of believers are

Deeper Revelations Of The anonting

gunning for the anointing directly from the Lord and in some cases they fail to realise that they could also easily tap into the anointing that is readily available from men and women of God from the previous generation. Metaphorically speaking, the anointing is the impartation of God's ability from God to man and then from man to man hence, it is possible for the anointing to flow from men of God in one generation to other men of God in the successive generation. That is why in the realm of the anointing, there is such a thing as a *continuity of the anointing"* throughout all generations. The nature of the operation of the anointing is such that it flows through *"spiritual fatherhood" and "spiritual sonship"*. Therefore learning how to tap into the realm of the anointing from previous generations will help continue building on the foundations laid by the previous generations just like Joshua took over the leadership Israel based on the principles laid by Moses.

There is what I call the *"genealogy of the anointing"*. As much as there is a blood line that runs through the Bible, from Abraham up to Jesus, there is also an anointing line that runs through from one generation to the other as the anointing is imparted. The anointing is transferred or passed on from one generation to the next. Therefore, we need to learn to draw from the men and women of God who have lived before us just like David learned to receive the anointing from Samuel and the generation before him. The Bible says in Samuel 16:13 that *Samuel took the horn of oil and anointed him in the midst of his brothers, and the Spirit of the Lord came upon David from that day forward.* In 1 Kings 19 when Elijah was told to go and get Elisha, God said that he would be the prophet in his place. When you look at men of God here and there you realize that when they die, the office remains but the vessels have changed. God doesn't want the vessels to change and the offices removed because the kingdom of God must go on. The vessels may change but the offices remain and maintained by different vessels under the same anointing or even greater anointing. By studying his story, we learn something about getting the anointing from the previous generation. Elisha did'nt let Elijah, the prophet out of his sight. He followed him closely, hence the same spirit got hold of him.

In the generation of Elisha, in 2 Kings 2, do you notice that when he was in battle, who were the people who told him about Elijah being taken away? It was not the prophet. It was the sons of the prophet. *Why sons of the prophet?* They were called sons of the prophet not in a literal sense but because they had inherited a prophetic anointing from the previous generation. *What happened to the fathers?* There is no record of their existence in the Bible, which implies that the Fathers were already dead hence the anointing was transferred to the sons. The sons of prophets had the same anointing the prophets had. They had acquired the prophetic anointing through coaching, mentorship and servant hood. And so by right, they were also going to be prophets. *The school of prophets* that Elisha ran was mostly from the new generation. Most of them were sons of the prophets. Paul's ministry took off because Barnabas ministry helped him? It was Barnabas who brought him to the apostles (Acts 9). It was Barnabas who brought him to the city of Antioch to start his ministry. Barnabas was the key in his life. In each one of our lives there is always a link and a key.

Some ministers who are stereotyped and not open to fellowship and associate with other bona fide fivefold ministers, end up the losers themselves. They would not receive measures of anointing from other ministries which would have added colour and diversity of operations to their anointing and methodology. For example, there are men and women of God who have lived in the previous generation whose books are still available for us to draw the anointing from. I'm talking about God' generals of the 20th century such as, Keneth Hagin, Oral Roberts, Smith Wigglesworth, Billy Graham, Kathrine Khulman, William Brahnam, John Wesley, Alan Allay, Martin Luther King II, John G. Lake, Watchman Nee and others whom through their ministry and writings influenced and laid a strong foundation for our generation. You see, *that same anointing upon these great men of God comes by association, environment, and influence.* Kenneth Hagin says those who worked closely with him had the same anointing on them that he had on him. In fact, there are some anointings in some ministries that have left him such that he doesn't even have them anymore but his workers got them! That's the way you get anointings. That is how Elisha got Elijah's mantle and a double portion of the prophet's anointing. *He followed Elijah closely hence the anointing flowed easily from Elijah to him. It is therefore an undeniable fact that* you get the same anointing by *association, environment,* and *influence hence if you want the same type of ministry someone else has, follow that ministry closely.*

We therefore need to draw from the generation before. That's the key. And we need to draw from that which is before us before we can go forward. There is a reason for it. If every one of us has to start fresh without the help of the other, we will never reach where we are. Suppose it takes forty years to develop a certain truth and an anointing. Then another person has to go through the same mistakes and they died without passing the secret to the next generation. The next generation starts afresh and after forty years they would still be where the previous generation was. But if they could pass it on, then the next generation can start off where the other generation left off. So, we have to learn to receive from that which was before us. We have to learn how to draw the anointing from others.

Deeper Revelations Of The anonting

Degree of Sensitivity and Receptivity to the anointing

It is a divine truth that the extent to which one is open to receive the anointing determines how much of it he can receive. One must be highly sensitive to the promptings and leadings of the anointing in order to receive greater measures of that anointing. At times the anointing that is at work might be for healing or deliverance hence one has to be sensitive to the nature of the anointing present at a particular time. It is not enough just to know when the anointing comes upon you but it is also important that you become sensitive to progressive anointings that continues to flow in our lives. Jesus functioned and flowed in the anointing and also determined how much anointing to flow in at a particular time and place. Sometimes when God tells Him to flow in a sign, He will demonstrate a sign. In Mark 5, *when the woman with the issue of blood for twelve years touched His garment, the anointing flowed out of Him and healed her.* Jesus knew that the anointing had flown through His life that is why he responded by saying *"Who touched me?"* In other words, He knew how the anointing came upon His life and how the anointing could flow out of Him. The fact that in Luke 4:18, Jesus said *the Spirit of the Lord is upon Him*, tells us that He knew the anointing was upon Him. He was announcing it. He was telling it to the people using scriptures from the prophet Isaiah that the anointing was upon His life for the people to freely make a withdrawal. It is for the people to exercise their faith, believe it, and then receive the anointing of God into their lives.

In the same manner when people are not sensitive to the anointing of God, they would not know what it is like when it is flowing. We have to learn to be sensitive to the anointing. God gives the anointing by measure to us. The anointing upon our lives is increased measure upon measure, as we prove faithful to the anointing. The fullest potential of the anointing we can aspire to in whatever office we stand in is the anointing without measure – the same as the anointing upon Jesus' life. That means if God called you to be a prophet, aim to reach the measureless anointing in that office. If God called you to be a teacher, aim for that. Seek the anointing upon your life to increase until it is measureless. When you move into the ministry of signs and wonders, you have to be very precise to follow instructions from God. As we move into the anointing, you have to move exactly as God showed you -no less, no more. There have been men and women who have moved into levels of anointing close to the level of Jesus Christ in the office God has called them. Every minister called by God should aspire to reach into that anointing without measure. However there are principles to move into that measureless anointing.

Frequency Revelator

Practising the presence of God

It is a divine truth that the anointing needs an atmosphere, hence in order for it to manifest it in greater measures, it has to be provoked or stirred up through a variety of ways for example through listening to anointed preaching, deep worship music, praying in the Holy Ghost, fasting, fellowship with the Holy Spirit, intense meditation and studying the word, preaching and exercising the word, and other diverse forms and practices of ministering to the Lord. And through such practises, it is possible for the presence of God to manifest in one's life 24/7. This is what we call *practicing the presence of God*. If you keep these tools strong all the time, you are immoveable. It must be understood that we are carriers of God's anointing hence, the presence of God that we accumulate at home through our everyday lifestyles is what we take to minister.

I am not talking about the general presence of God that is always with us whether you are in the super market or driving a car and you are generally aware that God is there but I'm talking about a realm when we enter into called the *Throne Room presence*. There is a presence called the outer court presence, then there is a middle court presence also called the Holy Place, then there is a presence in the Most Holy Place called the *throne room presence*. These are different realms of God's presence. And further out there is a general presence of God over His people. But the presence which we need to tap into in these end times is what I call *the Throne Room presence* and this is what we experience when we are catapulted right into the throne room in heaven to receive directly from God's hand.

Divine Exposure, experimentation & practical involvement in ministerial activities

It is an undeniable reality that the anointing comes through constant and progressive experimentation and practical involvement in ministerial activities. In other words, the more one is involved in ministering, the greater the volumes of the anointing released. Hence there is in the realm of the anointing, a dimension which I call *Testing the anointing*. This means practicalising the anointing, putting it into practical use or action. The reason why many people have failed to tap into greater measures of the anointing is because they just *talk about the anointing* but they don't *talk the anointing*. Talking the anointing means practically demonstrating it through miracles, signs and wonders such that the lives of people are transformed. Therefore,

Deeper Revelations Of The anonting

if you want to see your anointing increase to alarming and immeasurable proportions, don't just talk about it, instead demonstrate it. The common cliché held by dozens of people that *practice makes perfect* is actually a powerful spiritual principle that provokes greater volumes of the anointing to flow. This implies that active use of the anointing increases maturity hence you must exercise it to the fullest degree in your life!To illustrate the operation of the principle of testing the anointing, it is recorded in I Samuel 17:34 that David said to Saul, "

Your servant used to keep his father's sheep, and when a lion or a bear came and took a lamb out of the flock, I went out after it and struck it, and delivered the lamb from the mouth; and when it arose against me, I caught it by the beard, and struck and killed it. Your servant has killed both lion and bear; and this uncircumcised Philistine will be like one of them, seeing he has defied the armies of the living God.

Moreover, when confronted by the giant Goliath, David said, *"The Lord, who delivered me from the paw of the lion and from the paw of the bear, He will deliver me from the hand of this Philistine.* In other words, David was now basing his confidence in the anointing from the experience through *exercising the anointing.*

The bottom line is that you must test the anointing and be faithful to it at each level you have. You must test it against the lion and the bear before Goliath. It is God's method to always train us step by step. We are not running in the Spirit; we are led by the Spirit. We are to walk step by step. If David had to face Goliath before he learns to face the lion and the bear, he would never have been successful. The reason he was successful is because he has been training, practising and exercising the anointing. David had exercised the anointing that God has on him. In other words, his ability to conquer the lion and the bear is the result of the anointing and not on the result of himself. When the lion came for his lamb, he pounced on the lion and yanked the lion by the beard. He then came to the bear, one of the strongest animals and killed it. Having tasted that, when he looks at the Philistine, he was not relying on his own strength. He knew it has to be God. Who is this Philistine now? David had tested the anointing and brought victory for the whole tribe of Israel.

In a ministerial context, if you had not tested the Word of God in the fellowship of ten or thirty people, don't try to test it in a group of one thousand people. If you have not been faithful to learn to operate in prophecy in a home fellowship, don't try to test it in public. We have to learn to be faithful. And some of the ways we operated in the word of knowledge and the things of God we start operating in small group. That is where you are trained. Mind you, if you have only ten people and you say somebody here has a backache you could easily find out because you just have to ask ten guys. You have it. You learn from there and you learn to hear clearly. You learn from there and you grow from there. When you have tested it against the bear and the lion you are ready for the Goliath. God will not release you until you have done your time of training.

A Degree of consistency in exercising the anointing

In the realm of the anointing, there is a dimension which I call *maintaining the anointing*. The anointing must not only be received but progressively maintained. It must be understood that the nature of the anointing is such that it might not take abode permanently upon a vessel. It weans or lifts up especially when it's not utilised. It is therefore imperative that one maintains the anointing so that is does not lift up or wean continuously.

That is why some people attend some Christian conferences and were imparted some anointing by the anointed minister of God. They come back to their churches and they operate in the anointing for few months or so. After that, their anointing wane and they are back to their former selves. Actually, what happened is that these ministers did not know how to maintain their anointing by faithfulness in their communion with the Holy Spirit and in their prayer life. It must be understood that the anointing is not a once off event, it is not something that you only receive once in a life time when you have your annual conference; it is not something that you have to get only when you are sick or in trouble; instead it should be a continuous and progressive experience in a Christian's life. The bottom line is that if you don't guard jealously and maintain the anointing which you have received upon your life, you will loose it.

However, there is a certain spectacular dimension which one can reach whereby he becomes so infused into the anointing such that it becomes a permanent and indispensable part of his being. At that level the anointing would have so infiltrated the core of his being, saturated every fibre of your being such that it becomes your second nature and everything that you do, the anointing just naturally oozes out of you. This level comes though progressive, constant exercise, practice and activation of the anointing within you. *This is what I call practising the anointing.* Just like watering a plant in a garden, the anointing can be maintained through consistent prayer, study of the word, reading Christian books, meditation, fellowship and sensitivity to the Holy Ghost, praying a lot in tongues, ministering, having a constant flow of music, watching powerful DVDs of anointed man of God, watching anointed Christian television programmes, preaching and practically demonstrating what the word talks about.

Degree of graduation through progressive levels of the anointing

It must be understood that upon receiving an anointing, one must not remain at the same level. Instead, one must graduate or mature in the anointing from one level to the other just like we move from glory to glory, grace to grace and one level of faith to another. We all start with a measure of anointing God placed on our lives and then we grow from there. God is not going to give you the measureless anointing immediately. There must be testing; there must be proving and there must be faithfulness shown. God will give a deposit of anointing upon your life up to a certain level. Then as you are faithful to flow in it, as you are faithful to function in it, then God gives another measure. Then at that greater measure God will test your faithfulness. God will see whether you flow in it. What happens if you are not faithful? You remain at the measure you have been last given.

Let me illustrate with something you could identify with. Let's say that you have been given the measure of the anointing where you would be able to prophesy in public. However, every time the anointing and the Word of God came, you resisted it. Do not think that when the anointing comes, it is going to force you to do something. It does not force you. It just prompts you and the obedience must be yours. As the anointing comes, the person resists it the first time. Later in a different meeting, the same thing comes again. That person resists the prompting of the Holy Spirit again. That would be quenching the Spirit of God. That person can go on out of shyness, out of fear of publicity, out of whatever reason. He could justify his disobedience but that is not acceptable to God. He could give a natural reason and God would not accept it. The years could pass by and that person will still be the same. The measure of the anointing given to him was not allowed to function. The gift of God in such a person's life can never be perfected. You have to grow into the perfect operation of the gift. On the other hand, if the same person with the measure of anointing to prophesy publicly began to flow in that gift regularly whenever the anointing is there. Sooner or later, God is going to promote him or her. He is going to give you a greater measure of anointing to move into something else. God tests and proves us to know whether we are faithful or not. To illustrate how we progress or graduate in the anointing, David returned with his men to Judah after the death of Saul and was immediately recognized as King (2 Samuel 2:4). Then the men of Judah came and there they anointed David king over the house of Judah. For the first time he is recognized as king. Guess what? He was king only of two tribes. There were ten other tribes who were not in. It was later on that in 2 Samuel 5:1, that all the ten tribes of Israel came and in verse three they anointed David king over all of Israel. So his forty years reign was divided into 7/33. First seven years he was in Judah and the next thirty three years he had the whole of Israel.

Waiting for God's Timing in the anointing and understanding His times and seasons

The track record of David gives a good example of a practical model of how the anointing operates. He went through an eagle waiting period before he eventually became a King. In 1 Samuel 27:1 that's where the eagle comes in. David said in his heart, *"Now I shall perish someday by the hand of Saul. There is nothing better for me than that I should speedily escape to the land of the Philistines.* Why was this happening? See all the time when Saul was after him in I Samuel 22 to I Samuel 27, David's main lodging was in the cave. And in all those years he was in the cave, Saul was pursuing him. It was a waiting period that he really went through. *He had the anointing but no office while Saul had the office but no anointing.* Something has to give but it takes time to give. Saul reigned for forty years. David had a long waiting period. And even later when he moved into it, it was also a step by step. That's not very easy to be shut out outside a society, to be called a rebel, a reject of society. To have amongst your followers thieves and robbers. It is recorded in 1 Samuel 22:2, that *everyone who was in distress, everyone who was in debt, everyone who was discontented gathered to him.* He became captain like a pirate over these people. It's not very pleasant living in a cave, running away all the time but it was worth it. It was a trial and a waiting period.

In a ministerial context, if you are anointed, the gift will make room for you but it will take its time. You will be tested but it's where you would be like the eagle renewing your strength. You read about how successful he was in battle when he became king. *Do you know all his success when he was a king was the result of what he did while he was in the cave.* All this success came during the eagle period of David – the waiting. It's in that time that his army was actually built. God has strange ways to prepare us and it is not like what we would imagine. It was in his cave that he developed four hundred mighty

Deeper Revelations Of The anonting

men. Those thirty best men of his and those four hundred are the key generals in his army. And even later when he was in trouble it was these who backed him up. Where did he get these mighty men? In the cave and not in the palace. When he moved into the palace these four hundred men were behind him. I mean they have been through the thick and they are with him.

CHAPTER FIVE

THE REVELATIONAL SECRETS BEHIND MOVING IN GREATER DEPTHS OF THE ANOINTING

It is of paramount significance to unveil the divine truth that the anointing is the master key to unlocking the greater depths of the miraculous. In the realm of the anointing, revelation is the key that opens doors in the supernatural. If something is not yet revealed in the supernatural, it is a mystery. One can be a scholar who has studied the whole world and fathom all mysteries of the world but if the supernatural realm is not revealed to him, all his earthly knowledge is counted for nothing. The Bible says in 1 John 2:20 that *we have an anointing within us and we know all things.* This means that a person with the anointing knows all things. What does it mean to *"know all things?"* That speaks of *revelation knowledge, the knowledge that is revealed supernaturally without learning it.* That means the anointing opens the understanding of your inner man and causes you to fathom, comprehend and master all things in the supernatural realm. The Bible declares in John 16:13, that *when the Holy Spirit has come, He shall reveal all hidden secrets of heaven .* In the realm of the anointing, there are certain secrets that needs to be revealed to enable people to launch into the depths of God's power. There are certain hidden mysteries, divine truths, revelations and insights about the anointing that theologians and Bible scholars, ministers, pastors and believers across a broad spectrum of Christian faith have not yet fully comprehended. The key scripture that opens all other avenues of understanding is found in Isaiah 10: 27:

> *It shall come to pass in that day, that the burden shall be taken away from off thy shoulder, and his yoke from off thy neck, and the yoke shall be destroyed* **by reason of the anointing."**

This verse doesn't mean that the anointing breaks the yoke. Yes, the anointing breaks the yoke, but this particular portion of scripture lets us of the presence of the anointing, you can't be "yoked." When a yoke is placed on a Christian, it necessarily breaks off the anointing, because the Christian is anointed of the Lord. *'By reason of the anointing'* implies that the secret behind moving in greater depths of revelation, power, miracles signs and wonders is in *the anointing*. The secret, the key to all success, endeavours and power in life is in *the anointing*. If you want to win the whole world for Christ, just get the anointing and the world will be yours. The yoke of sickness or anything else that the devil tries to put on us will be destroyed *by reason of the anointing*, the dead are raised because of the anointing, and millions of souls shall be brought to the kingdom because of the anointing. *The secret is in the anointing.* The most powerful man in this world is the one who has greater volumes of the anointing. It is the anointing that makes a man to rule the world, impact lives, transform communities and leave an undeniable legacy in both the spirit and natural world. Everything revolves around the phenomenon of the anointing. Life is in the anointing. The anointing is the principal key, answer and solution to every challenge in every sphere of human endeavour. The following is a presentation of the key instructions or precautions for successfully moving in the anointing.

DIVINE REVELATIONS & SECRETS OF THE ANOINTING

It is highly imperative that during ministerial sessions you only do as occasion demands when the anointing is upon and within you.

The Bible unveils a very powerful and significant principle or spiritual law which lays a foundation upon which all other principles can be applied in the anointing. This principle is unveiled in 1 Kings 10:6, whereby Samuel instructed Saul saying,

"And then the Spirit of the Lord shall come upon you, and you will prophesy with them and be turned into another man. And let it be, when these signs come to you, that you do as the occasion demands; for God is with you.

This is the principle of ***"doing as occasion demands"***.

It is of paramount significance to unveil in this regard the divine truth that the way we operate in the anointing in the New Testament dispensation is somehow different from the way it was operated in the Old Testament dispensation. A historical background of the operation of the anointing in the past era will help reinforce a significant degree of understanding of this revelation. The reality is that folks in the Old Testament only received the *anointing upon* them and not *within* them hence, they had some restriction or limitations to operate only in specific times or moments as the Spirit leads. This is contrary to how we function in the anointing in the present time. In the New Testament dispensation, we have the liberty to move in both realms and dimensions of the anointing, which is the *anointing upon* and the *anointing within*, hence the principle of acting as occasion demands is interpreted slightly differently in our times. In other words it has a different meaning from what Old Testament folks would have it interpreted.

"Doing as occasion demands" does not necessarily mean acting only when one is prompted to, otherwise we would still be operating under the Old Testament covenant where folks were limited to operate anytime, anywhere and anyhow. What it basically imply for this generation is that you have the liberty to move and operate in the dimension of the anointing 24 hours a day. This is because if the *anointing upon* is absent as it comes and takes off, we can still tap into our inner resource and treasure which is the *anointing within*. Therefore, as far as the New Covenant of grace is concerned, there are no limitations, restrictions or constraints in the anointing, whatsoever. The Holy Spirit is the only yard stick to measure our performance, behaviour and conduct in the anointing.

Therefore, the phrase *"Do as Occasion demands"* means that you are required to move, operate or function in the anointing only when instructed to do so, only when a specific need or necessity arises or only when a direct instruction is given by the Holy Spirit. Only when a spiritual grace is made available for you to operate by the Holy Spirit can you move in the anointing. Only when the Holy Spirit comes, then you can do what the occasion demands. *Only when the anointing is stirred or activated from both within you and upon you can you do as the occasion demands.* In the absence of the anointing, one cannot do anything in a ministerial context. In other words, you only act when the anointing is *upon you* and *within you*. *If the anointing is not there, you cannot do what the occasion demands.*

This is a key spiritual principle that regulates the operation of the anointing. This implies that if the anointing does not come or there is no stirring from the anointing within and somehow you go ahead to do what the *occasion demands*, then it is not of God. That means you do only what you are told nothing less and nothing more. This is a powerful thing about moving in greater depths of the anointing of God. The bottom line is that the anointing must be available for any task to be undertaken and in the absence of its availability, it will make no effect.

To cement this revelation with reference to further practical evidence, in her biography, it is said that normally Kathryn Kuhlman would not minister in the absence of the anointing. Some people accused her of being long winded but she could not help it because if the anointing does not come, she cannot do anything. I have also heard of how William Branham could preach a sermon but he had to wait for the angel of God, before he could minister. The angel of God was the manifestation of his anointing on his life. After he preached, he walked up and down the stage waiting for the angel of God to come. For several minutes, he kept everybody waiting. Why, because he was waiting for the manifestation of the anointing. For him the anointing was the manifestation of an angel. This is to tell you how significant and integral it is to only do as the occasion demands when the anointing is available. If the anointing does not come, do not try to fake it because you won't be able to obtain any results.

To cement this revelation with reference to individual peculiarities and encounters in the realm of the anointing, I have also observed in my experience in the anointing that I only start writing books, teachings, devotionals and divine messages when the *revelation anointing* is present. If I attempt to write during any other normal day in the absence of the anointing, it would not work; instead, I would not receive even a single revelation of God's word. Only if that revelation anointing *comes upon* me or if I receive a stirring from the *anointing within*, will I start writing and in that way, a food of revelations will start to engulf and invade my spirit such that I can type on my laptop for the duration of the whole night or even for seven consecutive days. If not, then I would wait for the anointing to come. The same applies for the anointing to heal the sick, cast out devils or even raise then dead (*Resurrection anointing*). For example, if you just decide to bump into a mortuary and command the dead to rise in the absence of the anointing, you might be embarrassed because nothing might happen but if you receive that stirring from within you, which is the same Spirit that raised Jesus Christ from the dead, you will just point at a dead man and he will just jump out of the coffin and start running and praising God. This is such a powerful spiritual law and principle governing the operation of the anointing, especially for those who desire to move in greater depths of the anointing so that you are not hurt or frustrated when you operate in that dimension of the anointing of the Holy Spirit.

Heaven is legally bound to release anything demanded on earth under the anointing.

It must be expressly understood that after the natural realm was initially disconnected from the spirit realm as a result of the fall of Adam, man needed an *anointing* in order to move or operate in the supernatural In other words, it took the anointing for man to legally operate in the realm of the spirit. This means that the anointing is what brings both the realm of the supernatural and the realm of the natural into perfect synchronisation to function together in harmony to fulfil God's will and purpose. When the bible says *whatever you bind on earth shall be bound in heaven and whatever you release on earth shall be released in heaven*, it speaks of the manifestation of the harmony of both realms of existence. As a matter of fact the twin processes of *binding* and *loosing* comes through the anointing.

When the anointing of God is over your life, there are things that you say and do that carries the weight of God's power and obligates heaven to release whatever you place a demand on whether in season or out of season. Elijah tapped into this principle when he shut and opened heaven at his own prerogative. This is because heaven legalises, authenticates and certifies any demand placed upon it from the earth through the anointing. If anything is bound or released in the absence of the anointing, then it is rendered as illegal in the spirit realm hence, heaven will not be obligated to release it. That explains why some people have prayed and fasted, bound and loosed some things but they never came to pass because they lacked the missing element, which is the ingredient of the anointing. The greater truth is that any work performed in the absence of the anointing is not counted for anything in the spirit. On the other hand, every work done by men without the anointing is rejected by God. To cement this revelation with reference to scriptural evidence, Saul, who was anointed only as a king, was rejected by God when he offered the burnt offering because he was not anointed as a priest (1 Samuel 13:9-14). King Uzziah also tried to be a priest and judgement fell on him because he did not carry the priestly anointing (2 Chronicles 26:18).

As a matter of fact, according to spiritual laws of heaven, there are two principal forces by which a divine substance or blessing can be released from heaven and that is *through faith* and *though the anointing*. This implies that if you require anything in heaven, you can either acquire or place a demand for it through the *exercise of faith* or by the *release of the anointing* and both strategies work either way. The anointing is such a sacred divine substance that it causes all forces of divinity to work on our behalf. This is because it has such a strong, magnetic and attractive force that can cause the blessings

Deeper Revelations Of The anointing

in the spirit realm to manifests instantly in the natural. That is why a man with the anointing does not struggle to get results from the spirit realm.

The Anointing is the Key that Opens the Flood gates, Door of Heaven

==The anointing is the currency that regulates or governs the economy of Heaven==

There are certain divine truths which need to be unveiled through analogy by the use of physical phenomena so that you might catch an in-depth understanding of how the supernatural realm operates. Metaphorically speaking, *money is like a current, it's either flowing towards you or flowing away from you and that is why it is called a currency.* In the natural realm, money is the currency of every economy under heaven. However in the supernatural realm, the currency of the economy of heaven is the *anointing*. While we have the *dollar, rands, pula, euro, nairas* and many others as typical currencies of economies of this world, the currency of heaven is measured in *anointings*. For example a person could be having *one thousand anointings* in his heavenly bank account.

The use of this typological illustration is meant to cement and reinforce an understanding of how significant the anointing is as a divine substance in the economy of God. The anointing is what regulates the wealth of heaven. For anything to be authentic, legalised or approved in the Kingdom, it must have done through the *anointing*. Allegorically speaking, for any legal transaction or spiritual exchange between heaven and earth to be rendered valid, it has to be done though the *anointing*. The greater truth is that anything that is done in the spirit dimension through the anointing catches the attention of heaven hence, it becomes *God's business*. However, anything that is done outside the context of the anointing is regarded as a waste and is not counted for nothing in the supernatural. Instead, it is regard as religion. Religion is doing ministerial work using one's own ability outside the context of the Holy Ghost and the anointing. That is why the bible says at judgement *every man's work shall be tested by fire and anything that will not stand the fire will be burnt* (1 Corinthians 3:13).

In the context of this scripture, the *fire* speaks of the *anointing of the Holy Ghost*. This implies that any ministerial task, be it fasting, prayer, giving, preaching or anything that is not done though the *anointing* is counted as worthless in the supernatural. In other words, it doesn't carry any weight, value or substantial effect in the spirit dimension. This is because in his mortal state, man cannot successfully do what God has not *enabled* him to do. Man requires a divine enablement (*which is the anointing*) for him to operate successfully and effectively in the earthly realm. The reason why so many people are fasting, praying but they are not seeing results is because they are doing all these things in the *absence of the anointing*. If you engage in any of these spiritual exercises or activities without seeking for God's ability (*anointing*), God will just fold His arms and just watch how far you can go with your own strength and ability. Therefore, it is highly imperative that you check first if the anointing is available before you could undertake any of these spiritual exercises because everything has to be done *in the anointing*, *by the anointing* and *with the anointing* of the Holy Spirit for it to make a tremendous impact both in the natural and supernatural realms.

The anointing is a costly and precious spiritual substance and a currency that regulates the economy of Heaven; hence it comes with a price.

The anointing is not automatically given to anyone despite the level of calling upon his life. There is a price to be paid. It comes with a package. It must be understood that in the realm of anointing, there is no such thing as *automatic anointing*. Some say, "*If God has designed me to be an evangelist, then when the time comes for me to be an evangelist, I will be an evangelist. The evangelistic anointing will drop on me in whatever I do and wherever I am.*" I am sorry to say this but it will not happen. People called to be evangelists have lived and died without moving into that office. The anointing to operate in an office or ministry is not automatic. You may be called, chosen, and predestined to function in certain offices and ministries but the anointing is not automatic. Too many people are looking for automatic anointing. There is no such thing. There is a price to pay in order to get the anointing. Even when God has chosen and predestined you, the anointing is so precious that you must be tested before it comes on your life. Therefore, to make ourselves available is only half the story. When we avail ourselves, God tests us until we are ready.

The description of how the anointing is created in the natural from an optimum mixture of the best species of the land is ample evidence that portray how precious the anointing is as a heavenly commodity. As a result, the anointing is so highly valued, scared, special and delicate substance or divine commodity of heaven. Because of it nature, although is the New Testament dispensation God places the anointing upon everybody, greater depths and volumes of this precious substance are imparted upon those who would have passed a test. In this case, the anointing could be best described as God's supernatural ability that He imparts to His chosen ones who pass the test.

Deeper Revelations Of The anonting

That means you could have a prophecy hanging over your head that you are going to be highly anointed but if you don't pursue that ingredient of the anointing, it might not work out for you. There are things in life that are free but they are not cheap. They are free because somebody has paid the price. When I speak to many people who are coming up in the ministry, they have this idea that God's call will come in its own time, in spite of what they do. It will not. God will prove and test you and only when one passes His test, will the anointing come. What happens if they fail the test? They may live and die without entering and receiving the anointing. The anointing is so important since it makes you what you are. You can have a million people prophesy over you that you are a prophet. Pastors can lay hands on you until they leave their finger prints on your head or until your hair wear off from the crown of your head but it will not make you a prophet until the actual tangible anointing comes then you are one.

You may be predestined to be one but you are not one until the anointing comes and hit you and is imparted into your life. The anointing makes the difference. You could have a call of God to be an evangelist and you are doing all you can to get into that ministry. You could have the best mission board to support you. You could have arranged for twenty sponsors to support you financially and spiritually. You planned, write, begged or borrowed to get a place. You could knock on doors and beg to minister there. But if the anointing is not there, you could very well fold your ministry up like an umbrella and be kept aside. What is lacking is the anointing. The anointing makes you what you are in God's kingdom. It is very dangerous to move into any ministry without an anointing.

No man can successfully embark on the work of ministry without the anointing. There is no church without the anointing

The Bible presents a record of ordinary men who were not even known by anybody and did not occupy any centre stage in their generation but their story changed when they received the anointing. All of those men whom God had used had no ability in themselves until the anointing came. When the anointing came upon their lives, they could do things above and beyond their ability. The Anointing breeds popularity. The anointing is what reveals you, makes you famous and advertises the God in you. That is why a man with an anointing cannot be hidden no matter how humble he is. The reason why certain ministers like Pastor Benny Hinn, Pastor Chris, Oral Roberts, Kenneth Hagin and Kathrine Khulman, and may others took the centre of the world stage in ministry is because of the greater dimensions of the anointing they are operating in their lives. It's not because they can teach better than anybody else. As a matter of fact there are many great orators who can rant and rave in their preaching but they are not even known in their locality because they don't have the substance of the anointing.

No man can receive anything except it be given from above (John 3:27) and by the same token, no man can receive an anointing except it be given from above. In the absence of the anointing there is no such thing as the work of ministry because every ministerial work begins when one has received a divine enablement form God to effectively and efficiently undertake it. To cement this revelation with reference to scriptural evidence, Bezaleel and Aholiab received special skill in metal work, jewellery and embroidery (Exodus 31:1-6). Note how God attributes their ability, and those with them, to His anointing (Exodus 31:6). Moses and the seventy elders received special ability to govern and lead Israel (Numbers 11:16, 17, 25). Joshua received special wisdom (Deuteronomy 34:9). David's special ability as a mighty soldier and warrior came from the anointing upon his life (2 Samuel 22:33-35). It was not a natural ability but it was a supernatural impartation that trained his hands for war and his arms to bend a bow of bronze. Elijah and Elisha received the power to work miracles through the anointing upon their lives (2 Kings 2:9, 14). Daniel received supernatural understanding and wisdom through the anointing upon his life (Daniel 5:11). Jesus began His miracle ministry after receiving the anointing upon His life (Acts 10:38).

Any ministerial tasks conducted in the absence of the anointing are rendered null and void in the spirit realm

Any Christian who is involved in any kind of ministry, full-time or otherwise should be very much aware of the need for the Holy Spirit's anointing, both in his life and in those things which he seeks to do. Our benchmark and example to follow must always be Jesus Christ Himself. He made it plain to His disciples how important the Holy Spirit's anointing is in one's life. He said: *"It is the Spirit who gives life, the flesh profits nothing. The words that I speak to you are spirit, and they are life"* (John 6:63). What is Jesus saying? Simply this, that if we do not minister in the anointing of the Holy Spirit, we profit absolutely nothing! Outside of the realm of the Holy Spirit is the realm of the flesh. If we are not ministering in the realm of God's anointing we are attaining absolutely nothing of eternal value! Our efforts are fruitless and profitless. The Apostle Paul spoke it plainly: *"for the letter kills, but the Spirit gives life"* (2 Corinthians 3:6). To seek to minister to people outside of the anointing of God will defeat our purpose, as well as kill both our spirit and the spirit of those who hear us (*and that is very sad*). There is no place in our pulpits for anything but anointed messengers and messages. But alas, such a lot of what we hear today is nothing more than intellectual sermonizing and entertainment, a playing with words. God's Holy Spirit should be witnessed first and foremost through the minister and his ministry.

God jealously guards and takes a personal responsibility to safeguard and protects His anointing which He places upon His vessels

The anointing that God places on His vessels is so holy, precious and sacred as a heavenly commodity to the extent that God takes personal responsibility over His *anointing*. In other words, God means business with His anointing to the extent that He personally warned the authorities against touching His anointed ones. In 1 Chronicles 16:22, God strictly and specifically gave the instruction *"Touch not My anointed ones, do My prophets no harm"*. In other words, He made a sovereign declaration that under whatsoever circumstances, His *anointed* and *anointing* must never be touched, abused, prejudiced or sanctioned. As far as God is concerned, anybody else has the liberty to undergo any ordinary plight of humanity but those upon whom He has invested His interest, which is the anointing are exempted from undergoing harsh realities of human judgement.

In the context of the above mentioned scripture, while it might appear to casual readers of the word as if God is somehow protecting the interest of his servants from persecution by authorities, in actual fact, He is not protecting them as in their personal capacity. Instead, He is protecting or safe guarding His anointing upon them. That is why there is a huge supply of heavenly forces such as angelic beings released for men and women who are highly anointed by God. God allows his servants to go through persecution for them to carry a heavier weight of glory (2 Corinthians 4:17), hence He does not have a problem with any of them being persecuted for His sake. Therefore, it is clear that in this case He is not protecting them in their personal capacity although He provides His angels to protect us. Instead, He is safe guarding His anointing because it is a holy, sacred and a precious divine substance of heaven. By this statement, it doesn't mean that God is trying to stop people from persecuting saints, because the Bible says we must through many tribulations enter the kingdom. Instead, He is actually trying to protect the ordinary and ignorant people of this world from the danger of tempering with His fire, *the anointing* which He has placed upon

His servants. He is therefore alerting the ordinary people of the world to be careful lest they get burnt by the fames of fire that He has placed upon His anointed ones. It's like alerting a person to be aware of a dangerous animal in the neighbourhood. This is because many people of this world have died because they tempered with the *boiling anointing* that God put upon His servants. This is how God preserves the anointing across generations.

As a matter of fact, God takes no pleasure in those who disrespect His anointing upon His vessels. Miriam learnt it the hard way (Numbers 12:1-10). It is one sure way of making God angry. God watches closely over His servants because of His vested interest upon them – *the anointing of the Holy Spirit*, the most precious substance and holy heavenly commodity. That is why it is a very precarious move to challenge, oppose or stand in the way of the anointed because such people are heavenly guarded and protected by God, hence anything you say against them touches the apple of God's eye. Many, even believers have unnecessarily brought curses of judgement upon themselves because of standing against the anointed of the Lord.

There is a grace period for operating in the anointing with sin and it is extremely dangerous to sin with the anointing.

It is very dangerous to mess with the anointing. Playing with the anointing is like playing with fire because the repercussions are severe. Saul was condemned and rejected by God because he wanted to move or operate in the priestly anointing by offering a sacrifice when he was not a priest. Uzzah died on spot when he accidentally touched the ark of God's anointing. Both Eli's two sons died when they were moving in the priestly anointing in sin, despite being warned by God not to. Ananias and Saphirah died in the presence of God because they lied to the Holy Spirit, the operator behind the anointing. The reason why instant judgement was instigated against this couple is not necessarily because they lied per se, since many people lie almost every day but they are not killed. The greatest outrage was that they *lied in the presence of God's anointing*.

In other words, from a spiritual point of view, they were playing or moving in the anointing with sin. How do I know that they tried to operate in the anointing with sin? This is because the Bible says there was a strong *prosperity anointing* that was moving as believers gave everything that they had and *there was no poverty amongst them*. To move in the anointing does not necessarily mean healing the sick and casting out devils. There is an evidence in this case that there was a *prosperity anointing* which the Holy Spirit had released and every believer was trying to move in that *prosperity anointing* including Saphirah and Ananias. Although in the New Testament dispensation there is a grace period given for operating in the anointing without any instant judgement, God still demands accountability over every task performed in the anointing. Some ministers have not learnt to harmonize the two natures in them. On one hand, they desire to serve God but on the other hand, they have not died to their flesh. They may have paid the price to secure some levels of anointing by earnest and constant praying and fasting. However, they have not taken care to uproot strongholds from their flesh. In the weaker and unguarded moments of their private lives, they give in to their strongholds and indulge in secret sins. This is not how we should operate in the anointing.

The anointing exhibits its own unique personality which might be different from that of a vessel.

It must be expressly understood that the fact that someone is moving in the anointing does not necessarily mean that anointing has to flow with his personality, character or behaviour. Instead, the anointing has its own unique and distinct personality and character which might be different from your usual personality. Hence, in the realm of the anointing, there is such a thing called *"The personality of the anointing"*. Some folks inadvertently presume that the anointing will automatically work with their personality but the truth is that it may be different from your personality. In some instances, depending on the gravity, magnitude or degree of manifestation, it might even assume a character that is completely diametrical from yours. In this case, it can seem like two different personalities fused in one body. It must be expressly understood that by description, *the anointing is the supernatural ability imparted by God to a yielded human vessel to perform His task*. The reality is that when that impartation comes, there is a definite change that is involved. It could change you to a totally different person.

Therefore, the onus is in your hands to learn how to harmonize the two personalities together and let it flow as one. It can be like having two personalities. Now, the anointing is like another factor working inside you, speaking to you, influencing your life, when it comes upon your life. It's a tremendous factor that can influence your life. It is sometimes like another person's voice speaking in you. The anointing depends on the degree your personality yields to the Holy Spirit. The anointing and the personality will appear to be diametrically opposing. Many folks have a wrong picture of the anointing. They always think that the anointing has to flow with their personality. It does not have to. Your anointing may be an indication of your personality but it does not have to because the anointing has the power to *turn you into another person*. When it does, you still have your personality and you have to differentiate between the two. Samson was a powerful man under the anointing but when the anointing was not there, he was easily influenced, easily falling for women because he did not know how to rein over his personality and subject it under his anointing.

A significant degree of liberty, freedom, discretion or prerogative is given to you to move within the framework of the anointing.

Sometimes God does not give you any specific instruction regarding how you should operate in the anointing and that gives you some freedom to move according to a style comfortable to you. When the anointing of the Spirit of God is there, whether you shout or speak softly, it works any way. That is an interesting part about God's anointing. When you are possessed with the anointing of God, you are given certain liberty. Here is where we have to be careful about passing judgments on some ministers' styles of ministering under the anointing. Some may be flamboyant and may take their coats off and wave them at people and they start falling left and right. Some may be stiff, glued to the pulpit, speak in a monotonous tone and are downright boring. In either extreme of personal styles, if the anointing is there on their lives, they will still do God's work. Within the liberty is what I call personal preferences and personal styles. What happen if people do not differentiate between the personal style and preferences and the actual anointing? Many people think that when the anointing comes on a man of God, they become robotic, that every move and word they make or say is from God. No, it is not so. A certain amount of liberty is given to you to channel the anointing of God. When the Spirit of God and the anointing of God rise within your life, you have a certain amount of free will or movement within a certain boundary.

That is why there is such a thing as *creativity in the anointing*. This is manifested through the method used to channel the anointing in a specific direction. It must be understood that God is creative and in every generation, He ushers new waves of the anointing so that His work is current, dynamic

Deeper Revelations Of The anonting

and more appealing to His people. Therefore, believers must be open to the new, creative and dynamic ways of moving in the anointing. For example, it does not necessarily mean that you will move in the anointing in the same way as Kenneth Hagin, Kathrine Khulman or Oral Roberts although they were heavily anointed by God. This is because there might be something new, unique or distinct which God is currently unveiling in this generation which requires a completely different methodology or approach to operating in the anointing. For example, during the word of faith movement, multitudes of people used to be healed by faith without any visible or tangible manifestations. However, it is a current norm in every sphere of Christian realm in our generation that the move of the anointing is always accompanied by diverse manifestations such as people falling under the power, laughing in the spirit or shaking hysterically whenever the anointing is administered.

It suffices to say that if you want to see what God is doing in a particular generation or dispensation, just watch how His anointing operates worldwide, the direction the anointing is taking on a global scale and you will catch a glimpse of what He is doing in the supernatural realm. The move of the anointing is what determines the direction of the work of ministry. That is why you don't receive a ministry prior to receiving an anointing but you receive the anointing first so that you can move in a specific direction to mark in the work of ministry. The Bible speaks of the sons of Issachar who had an acute understanding of the times and seasons of God and new exactly what Israel ought to do in a particular season (1 Chronicles 12:32). The question is: How did they know the seasons? Did they have calendars which accurately showed them the way to go? Definitely not! I guess besides having a supernatural revelation, they got some of their direction by analysing and looking at the operation of the anointing in their generation. The anointing acts as a guide or campus to show us what God is currently working on in the supernatural.

Overstepping the line in the realm of the anointing has far reaching spiritual repercussions or consequences.

It is of paramount importance to highlight as a word of caution that while the anointing is the most sought after and most celebrated divine substance in the universe, using it unceremoniously has severe consequences. As a result of misconduct in the anointing, some ministers have been afflicted by some sicknesses and even departed to be with the Lord before their time and others have gone to the extent of insanity just like the condition of Saul after loosing the anointing. One of the laws of operating in the anointing is to know the limitations of the level and type of anointing God called you to so that you do not to overstep your boundary. For example, if you are called to be a prophet and you try to be a teacher, you enter the permissive will of God.

For example, it is said that Kathryn Kuhlman towards the end of her ministry, her anointing seems to have stopped in her services, and she also suffered from cancer and despite many anointed men and women of God praying over her, she was not healed. The reason why the anointing stopped towards the end of her life and ministry was because God wanted her to retire and spend her remaining years with Him. However, she still insisted on serving God despite the anointing being stopped. When she persisted in her wilfulness, the Lord had to allow cancer to afflict her in order to slow her down. That was why she was not healed, despite being visited by so many anointed men and women of God. In Kathryn Kuhlman's case, the anointing was lifted up in her later years to enable her to take a rest from her ministry. Unfortunately, she did not heed the Lord's request, and the enemy took advantage of the situation by placing some sickness upon her. As the anointing was already lifted up from her, there was no more anointing to break the yoke of sickness upon her. God is always gracious to His servants. After labouring so many years for Him, God may grant a period of rest to His servants to spend time with Him before they depart from this earth. However, some do not take heed to God's desires and in the end, are afflicted with sicknesses and diseases.

The anointing operates according to the law of grace and works regardless of the vessel's weaknesses or state of imperfection.

It must be expressly understood that there are vast differences between operating in the dimension of the anointing and operating in the dimension of the glory. The realm of glory is a realm of perfection therefore, when operating in that dimension, God strictly demands the highest levels of consecration, hence all your weaknesses, mistakes and faults are non-operational. In other words, it is virtually impossible to operate in the dimension of glory with any imperfections because it is a realm of perfection. However, operating in the realm of the anointing is a slightly different story altogether in the sense that one does not need to be perfect in order to move in the anointing. God requires more of your availability than perfection so that He can place His ability on you. The realm of glory is a realm of perfection because God does everything by Himself. However, in the realm of the anointing, He needs a man so that He can place His ability on him. Therefore, the glory is correspondingly to God what the anointing is to man.

However, some folks who do not have an in-depth understanding of the anointing inadvertently presume that a person really has to be that perfect before he can receive the anointing. Consequently, many have restricted or placed limitations upon themselves from tapping into greater depths of the anointing because they thought that one qualifies to enter such realms though perfection instead of grace. If the anointing were to be given to only perfect people, then there would be no one who is anointed in this world because every person to a certain extent exhibits a certain degree of weakness. The greater truth is that the anointing operates regardless of the person's faults, imperfection and weaknesses because it is governed by *the law of grace*. It must be understood that while the callings and gifts of God are irrevocable, the anointing to enable them to operate this gifts can be uplifted. There is however a grace period for people to operate in that state of weakness under the anointing before God takes action.

It is recorded in I Samuel 11:6, that Saul would move in the anointing despite the fact that he was in a fit of anger. When the Spirit of God came on Saul, he began to show traits out of character with his personality. Whether he was in perfect or imperfect state of emotion, he still operated in the anointing. It is recorded that *the Spirit of God came upon Saul when he heard the news, and his anger was greatly aroused*. That tells me that the rest of the things he did had some anger involved yet in spite of that God still works. God works in spite of the anger that Saul had. It was the same way with Samson. Samson did certain things that were not from the Lord but when the anointing of God came upon him, he was able to work mighty exploits. However, the fact that the anointing operates according to God's grace does not mean that people should take advantage and sin purposely knowing that they will just move in the anointing because there will be consequences as I have indicated before.

In the realm of the supernatural, it is possible for the anointing to be given or released upon a vessel and be taken away.

It is a divine truth that although the gifts of God are irrevocable, the anointing to function in those gifts however can be lifted. In other words the anointing is not a permanent divine substance but takes a temporary residence as it comes upon yielded vessels and then takes off as God wills. The reason why the anointing temporarily comes and then takes off is because many are not yielded completely to the leadings of the Holy Spirit. God will not release an anointing beyond the level of your spiritual capacity or receptivity otherwise the anointing will choke you. In the realm of the anointing, God will go along with your level. He may ordain that you function in that certain level of anointing but if you ever say, *"Lord I cannot do it,"* He could easily get someone else to do that task because nobody is indispensable. It's a dangerous thing to ever think that we are indispensable because God could easily get somebody else.

To cement this revelation with reference to scriptural evidence, we see this in effect in the life of Saul. When Saul was not very faithful, he lost his anointing. The Bible says *God latter rejected him as a king*, hence the kingly anointing that goes with that kind of responsibility was lifted from him and it latter rested on David. But how did he loose his anointing? By first loosing his office. Spiritually speaking, if you lose your office, it means you lose your anointing because it's the anointing that establishes the office. You don't have an office without an anointing in God. Judas Iscariot by betraying Jesus also lost his apostolic office and the anointing associated with that office and Matthias replaced him. When Moses was feeling the pressure of judging the Israelites on their way to Canaan, he came to a point where he said, *"Lord, I cannot take it anymore."* And although the anointing was not taken away from him completely, it was divided and transferred amongst the seventy leaders who operated under him. In other words, there was a portion of the anointing that was taken away from him hence he functioned less in that dimension because he told God he could not take it anymore.

This explains why some men of God operated in higher dimensions of the anointing especially at the beginning of their ministries but then it appeared somewhere towards the end of their career that they no longer functioned in those realms. This is because many would have lost the anointing either due to unfaithfulness or other reasons known to them and God. Therefore, the anointing must be treasured, cherished, natured, maintained and protected because you can loose it anytime. Unlike the gifts of the spirit which are irrevocable, the anointing is not something that when you receive it, you are guaranteed of operating in it for ever. This is because its existence and ability to continue operating in your life depends to a larger extent on how you manage it, maintain it, cultivate it and protect it.

There is an intricate connection between the calling and the level of anointing one exhibits. The level of anointing upon a vessel is an indication of the calling upon his life.

Deeper Revelations Of The anonting

Contrary to how the worldly system operates, whenever God puts you into a position of authority, He makes sure that you have an anointing that equips you to function in that particular office or position. The greater truth is that God will never put you into a position without the anointing and ability. This is because the measure of anointing which God places upon a vessel is directly proportional or tantamount to the level of his calling. Hypothetically speaking, the man who cleans a yard at home does not have the same authority as a principal in a school because of the nature of their work. The principal will require more authority and power because of the responsibility which he has or the office which he occupies. Therefore, the greater the calling, the higher the level of the anointing one can receive from God. For every promotion that you receive in your office from God, there is a directly proportional increase in the anointing. Therefore, you cannot separate the *anointing* from an *office* because these two goes hand in glove. That is why if you loose your office, you also loose the anointing that goes with occupation of that office.

In the natural, if a manager resigns from his post, he looses the authority and power associated with that position. If he comes after his resignation and orders his subordinates to undertake certain tasks, they can only just stare at him but would not listen or take any instructions from him anymore. Why? Because he does no longer have the authority and power that goes with occupying that office. By the same token if a man looses an office, he also looses the anointing to function in that office. Therefore, if you loose your office, the anointing to function in that office will automatically be lifted off you.

If you want to grow in the anointing ... use what you've got.

Progressive Growth and graduation in the anointing comes through faithfully moving in the measure you already have

It is of paramount significance to unveil the divine truth that faithfulness, obedience and humility are the most integral and fundamental principal pillars when it comes to successfully operating in greater depths of the anointing. The underlying principle is that unless we are faithful to what we already have, more will not be given. To cement this revelation with further scriptural evidence the bible says *He that is faithful in least shall be faithful in much* (Luke 16:10; 19:17). In other words, if you are faithful to move and flow in the anointing that God has given you, God will grant more anointing in your ministry. *Therefore, progressive growth and graduation in the anointing comes through faithfully moving in the measure you already have.* Being faithful with whatever gifts or ministry that God has placed in us that will provoke an even greater, deeper and higher dimension of the anointing in our lives. Elisha was faithful for about ten years serving Elijah. In fact, he was known as the one who poured water on Elijah's hands (2 Kings 3:11) and he got the prophetic anointing in a double measure.

In a ministerial context, for example, if you receive a word of knowledge but then you decide to resist giving them since you would rather just preach and teach. Perhaps it is in a home fellowship or in a smaller meeting and the word of knowledge comes to you. You resist giving the word in fear that nobody responds. The danger is that there is a possibility that you can remain that way for the next ten years until you obey. But when you obey and you are faithful in that gift, a greater measure of that anointing will develop in your life. You could flow into an even greater measure of the anointing. It will grow from measure to measure, faith to faith and glory to glory. Hence, we must grow until we arrive at the perfect function of a ministry that God has for us.

Alternatively, God could give you a ministry of prophesying over people and every time the anointing comes, you could sense God telling you to act on the prompting. However, all these things need a human response. You may say, *"No, I do not want to do that. I do not feel like doing that."* You resist and you quenched the Spirit of God. If you keep on doing that, ten years later you will still be where you are. You would not have progressed but you are still stagnant in one place. If you are not even faithful to the measure God gives to you, there is no point in talking about the measureless anointing. Unless you are faithful to the measure God gives you will not have more.

For example, when God first started operating the word of knowledge in my life, I had to faithfully give it. When it comes, I will say, *"All right God is showing that this is the category of the sickness He wants to heal,"* and I faithfully gave it. Whether people respond or not, that is their responsibility. Whether you respond or not is your responsibility. You have to faithfully give it. I found something started happening. The more I give, the more it came. The more it came and the more I give out, it gets sharper and sharper. As I continued in it, later, I found out that it began to operate with another side effect. At first it operates with what I call the side effect of tangibility. I sense it on my body. Later it operates together with vision. It reached a certain point where it started operating with vision. When that operates with vision, it reaches a greater form of accuracy that can take place. That comes because of faithfulness.

Deeper Revelations Of The anointing

The anointing can be measured, implying that it can either be increased or decreased based on faithfulness and consistency in usage

It must be expressively understood that in the same way we measure a liquid substance in the natural, the anointing can also be measured as a spiritual substance. The principle of measuring the anointing implies that it can either be increased or decreased. The bottom line is that the anointing could be measured. Elisha had a double portion of Elijah's spirit (2 Kings 2:9). Note that the miracles recorded of his ministry exactly doubled that of Elijah. Elijah performed eight miracles while Elisha performed sixteen which is exactly the double measure of what Elijah did. This record of an exact double portion of miracles in Elisha's life shows us that Elisha functioned in twice the power that Elijah had. This is an undeniable or irrefutable evidence that the anointing can be measured and that the greater the measure of the anointing upon our lives, the greater the ability to perform miracles, signs and wonders.

The greater truth is that every believer has a measure of the anointing upon their lives. To cement this revelation with reference to scriptural evidence, John affirmed in 1 John 2:20 that *yee have an unction (anointing) from the Holy One and you know all things*. And he continued to elaborate in depth in 1 John 2:27 *that the anointing which you have received of Him abides (lives, remains, dwells) in you."* He continues to unleash the revelation of the power of operating in the anointing by declaring in 1 John 4:4 that *"Yee are of God, little children, and have overcome them, because greater is He that is in you, than he that is in the world."* Moreover, in a related scripture, John strongly contends that *I can do all things through Christ that strengthens me (*Philippians 4:13*)*. Note that in the context of this scripture Paul is not talking about Christ *(the person)* but Christ *(the anointing)* that is resident in his human spirit. If he were referring to Jesus Christ, he would not have addressed him as *"that"*. It can therefore be concluded that Paul is talking about Christ, which is the anointing resident in us. Therefore, philosophically speaking, a man with an anointing can do anything to the extent of just lifting the whole world with the tip of his figure.

The greater truth is that just as we grow from faith to faith, from glory to glory, and from grace to grace, we also can grow in the level of anointing in our life. In addition, the Holy Spirit is received in measures. We can measure the amount and the level of anointing that operates in our life. There are different degrees and measures of the anointing. That measure of the anointing we are talking about here now is the measure of the anointing that God gives you to operate.

As you progress through the anointing, you must be able to measure and trace your record of graduation in the anointing from the time you started up to the level where you are.

The following are indications that one is ready to move to a higher level of new anointing: God will change your relationships, usher a new spiritual diet, and create a new hunger for the supernatural that will never be easily satisfied

"I'm giving you a new voice"

It is possible for one to graduate through different levels of the anointing in the same office.

It is important to highlight that upon reception of the anointing, God does not want us to stay at the same level of anointing for ever. As a matter of fact the anointing was originally designed in such a way that it has to flow like a food, a river of waters. In other words, it should continue to increase and food our spirits until we are saturated with high volumes of the anointing such that moving, functioning and operating in the anointing becomes our second nature. This is the essence of the anointing. On that note, it is therefore possible to graduate through different levels of the anointing even in the same office. This means that you could be a prophet and be anointed over and over again in different prophetic realm. You could also be an apostle and be anointed in different apostolic realms.

The fact that you are anointed does not necessarily mean that you have the anointing for everything, otherwise you run the risk of being a jack of all trades and a master of none. Many believers inadvertently presume that they have the anointing for everything, hence they run around attempting to do everything yet they end up not making any significant impact in the spirit realm and in their generation. The greater truth is that although God can give you different anointing to function in different offices, in most cases, He anoints you repeatedly such that you graduate through different levels in the same office. This is what I call *specialisation of the anointing*. For example, David was called to be the king but it happened that he was anointed twice in the same office. He was first anointed to be the king of Judah and then he was finally anointed to be the king of Israel but this time it was at a different level of anointing. *This implies that you can enlarge, increase, and multiply your anointing, tenfold, twenty fold, even up to a hundred fold in the same office.*

Deeper Revelations Of The anonting

Progression to higher dimensions of the anointing comes with new responsibility in the Kingdom

It is important to unveil the divine truth that higher dimensions of the anointing comes upon the acceptance of a new responsibility. When a Christian accepts a new responsibility, he should be anointed by the Holy Spirit for that task. Therefore, heaven is obligated to release a higher dimension of the anointing to enable him to function effectively at the level or realm which the new responsibility demands. For example, when a pastor is called to a new church or when a believer is chosen to be a music director, a departmental superintendent or an usher, he should be anointed by the Holy Spirit. Any new task to which a child of God is chosen and any new responsibility that God has given to him is so important that the Holy Spirit should anoint him upon the assumption of his new responsibility. Likewise, as the Christian ministers and continues to fulfil the work to which God has called him, he should constantly be being filled with the anointing.

This anointing is appropriation; it equips one for a task. When God calls, He qualifies, He equips and He prepares. Therefore when a Christian is called to a new responsibility, he needs to be equipped. He needs to be anointed by the Holy Spirit as God appropriates to him what he needs to fulfil his new calling and equips him for that calling. Therefore, if you want to determine the size of your calling, ministry or the responsibility God has given you, simply look at the measure of the anointing that God has put in your life. The truth of the matter is that the measure of the anointing upon your life is directly proportional to the size of your vision. Philosophically speaking, the larger the vision, the greater the measure of the anointing.

The anointing is governed by spiritual laws and principles and all ministerial activities are executed within the framework of the availability of the anointing.

Some people inadvertently presume that they will move or operate in any dimension of the anointing anytime, anywhere and anyhow. While such a notion might be partially true considering the nature of the end time dispensation into which we have been ushered, it suffices to highlight that there are parameters and principles to be followed when operating in the anointing. God is not a God of lawlessness, hence He has established His spiritual laws and principles to govern both the natural and spiritual realm. Hence, the anointing has it own parameters. It must be expressly understood that the anointing operates within the framework or context of God's word and it never contradicts the written Word of God under whatever circumstances.

Breaking the rules of the game when operating in the anointing can culminate in far reaching spiritual consequences. The Bible records in 1 Samuel 13:8-9 that Saul waited seven days for a sacrifice to be made before going to war, according to the time set by Samuel and when Samuel did not come to Gilgal, and the people were scattered from him. So, Saul said, *"Bring a burnt offering and peace offerings here to me,"* and he offered the burnt offering. However, God did not approve Saul's offering. But why was it not possible for Saul to make that sacrifice when in 1 Samuel 10:7, Samuel gave him the allowance for that? Why is it that in I Samuel 10:7, Saul was told to *'do as the occasion demands'* and here he did whatever the occasion demanded at that time and it was considered a wrong thing when he did everything possible to help the situation?. When Samuel came after Saul made his sacrifice, he gave him a strong rebuke. Why? The answer is simple. *The written law the Word of God in Saul's time did not permit him as a king to offer sacrifices, even though he had the Kingly anointing.* In other words, Saul attempted to operate in a different office (*priestly*) without the anointing to function in that particular office. The anointing is what legalises or authorises you or gives you permission to function in a particular office hence any attempt to move in an office without a corresponding anointing is deemed as illegitimate in Heaven, that is why Saul's case was regarded as a serious offense by the court of heaven. Moreover, even though I Samuel 10: 7, says *"do as the occasion demands,"* it takes for granted that you understand that it is within the context of the Word that we move in the anointing. Doing as the occasion demands does not mean that you go against the written Word and do as you please. It is through this conduct and act of disobedience that costed Saul his anointing, Kingly position of authority and eventually his life.

Moreover, some people think that just because they are anointed, they will do as they please and use the anointing for whatever they deem necessary. Hence, there is in the realm of operating in the anointing, such a thing as *"merchandise or commodification of the anointing"*. Some get involved in unhealthy relationships, manipulates people to give them money and some purports to have heard God instructing them to demand material possessions from people and all this is done under the pretence of the anointing. Hence in the realm of anointing there is such a thing as *manipulation of the anointing"*. In the case of Saul, he failed to recognize that he must wait for the anointing to come upon him and that *the anointing does not give you permission to contradict God's Word.* In other words, if the anointing is on your life and if you are a man, it does not give you permission to lay hands on a woman's sensitive parts. If you are a woman, it does not give you permission to lay hands on any part of a man that would embarrass him. Having the anointing does not give you the license to contradict the Word. You cannot give an excuse that you were operating under the anointing of God. The anointing will change your personality and you have certain liberty to operate a certain context but there are boundaries set by the written Word.

God demands completes sensitivity and obedience to peculiar instructions given by the Holy Ghost to function in the anointing

It must be expressly understood that when operating in the anointing, the fact that God has used you to move in a certain dimensions or direction today does not necessarily mean that you will move in the same way tomorrow. The move of God cannot be calculated, estimated or quantified because God cannot be put in a box. That is why there are divergent moves of the Holy spirit, depending on the nature of His operation, today He might breath upon the congregation as a mighty wind of power but tomorrow He might fall like rain or fire or earth quake but the truth of the matter is that He does not manifest in a similar fashion everyday but flows differently depending on what he is working at a particular point in time. That is why ministers are expected to be vigilant and open to a million ways of the move of God' Spirit so that they are not left on a spot while God had already moved forward and is doing something else. Sensitivity to the current operations of God's Spirit is therefore such an important key to moving in the anointing. This is because if you miss the Holy Spirit, you have already missed the anointing that comes with Him.

Moreover, it is highly imperative in order for us to move in greater dimensions of the anointing that we be sensitive to the instructions given by the Holy Spirit during ministerial sessions. At times when God's ability is working through your life, you may do things you would normally never do for they are foreign to your character. His instruction sometimes makes you function beyond your personality. The Holy Spirit does not limit to just your personality but beyond your personality. Sometimes He tells you to shout. It may not be your nature to shout but then you have to shout because He tells you to shout. For some other people they are just looking for the time to shout. Their personality is rather loud and glitzy and they would love to shout anytime. However, the Spirit of God may tell them to whisper, which is foreign to their personality. Is that possible? Yes. The Lord told Moses to take the rod and hit the rock. He hit the rock and the water came out. Then the next round the Lord told Moses to speak to the rock. Moses hit the rock instead of talking to it because he was now used to the way God moves yet God this time had a different methodology to get his job done. Such a conduct is what costed him the Promised Land. Isaiah was told to walk barefoot for three years and wear torn clothes. To an ordinary person this does not make sense but under the anointing you have to do as occasion demands. Kenneth Hagin says there are times when the Holy Ghost instructed him to hit some people who were on the prayer line on their bellies and when he obeyed, they were instantly healed. Smith Wigglesworth moved in a similar fashion and obtained alarming results of success. For example under the anointing, he would drag a dead body out of a coffin, point at it and command it to walk. Strange as it might sound, the dead man would surely be raised back to life in this way.

The anointing is what connects us to the realm of God's glory

From my experience in the realm of the anointing, I have observed that if you progressively continue operating in the realm of the anointing, you will end up reaching a dimension whereby you are just translated into the realm of the glory. The Bible makes it clear that in our walk with God, we move from faith to faith, grace to grace, glory to glory and from one level of the anointing to the other. However there are times when we are just catapulted from the realm of the anointing into the realm of glory. There are times when you are operating in the realm of the anointing and suddenly you feel like you are no longer operating in that realm anymore. It's as if there is a shifting in the spiritual atmosphere that has taken place in that realm and something completely brand new and different has been ushered. It's like shifting from driving a manual car into an automatic car.

At that level, you start feeling God's emotion through the anointing. That is why under an anointing you can feel God's emotion to a certain extent. For example, under the anointing you could sometimes feel a greater special love for people. Outside of the anointing, you do not feel as much. This is because the glory of God would have taken over to launch the people into an even greater realm of creative miracles. This is what Kathryn Kuhlman described in her biography as, *"A Glimpse of Glory."* When she is under the anointing and she sees a sick person like a sick child the feeling inside her is so immense that she feels like she could give her life so that this child could live and she dies. That is not a natural human emotion. There is something else coming out now through the being of a person. This is the dimension of glory. That is why there is an emphasis for a transition from the realm of the anointing into the realm of glory. Enock walked in this realm and he was translated straight into heaven. Philosophically speaking, he initially moved and operated in the realm of the anointing, graduated into even higher levels, greater depths and deeper dimensions in that realm until he was catapulted into the realm of glory, and he continued progressively functioning and excelling in that realm of glory until he was further translated into heaven. This is what we mean by a progressive transition from the *realm of the anointing* into *the realm of glory*.

The anointing makes a permanent dwelling on earth upon its release from the spirit realm

The anointing was made for earth and not Heaven. It is the only divine substance that can have a permanent dwelling in the earthly realm. Other divine substances do not permanently dwell on the earth. Once they are released from heaven, they can linger on the earthly realm for some time and once the purpose for which they were released is accomplished, they return to the spirit realm. But the anointing lingers permanently in geographical places, on churches, houses, streets, and people depending on the degree of manifestation. It works opposite to how manna was released. It was only released during a specific time and after that it disappeared. Manna typified the divine provision of God which would not only fall on the ground but on humans to quicken them to do his work.

It is possible for one to loose the anointing but still retain an office

It must be expressly understood that a call does not mean an anointing automatically. A call means an office. But the anointing may leave the office. You do not lose your call. The calling and the gifts of God are without repentance. But the anointing may not be there. The anointing will be there as long as the other laws are followed but on you personally the anointing may not be there. Sometimes people have used their office without the anointing. And it still works because of the faith level of people. But for it to function perfectly, you need the office to function with the anointing. To substantiate my view with reference to scriptural evidence, it is recorded in I Samuel. 1:13 that Hannah spoke in her heart; only her lips moved, but her voice was not heard. Therefore Eli thought she was drunk. So Eli said to her, *"How long will you be drunk? Put your wine away from you!"* Hannah said she is not drunk she is sorrowful. Eli then pronounced a blessing by saying, Go in peace, and the God of Israel grants your petition which you have asked of Him." The moment Eli said it, it was done. Who was Eli? Eli wouldn't be one of those priests you say was anointed. But he was in office as a priest. He had no anointing but because of his position and his office, his pronouncement released the blessing. He was not even operating in the anointing but when he pronounced a blessing, it was done. Why? Because he had an office even though he had lost his anointing.

When you have an office and a call, people who look up to your office and position and call can tap on your exousia without *dumanis*. There is *exousia* power and *dunamis* power. *Exousia* is power by authority. *Dunamis* is power by content. So here is Eli one of the fattest men in the Bible. His mere words carry enough authority to gladden the heart of a sorrowful woman praying for a child. But in actual fact he has lost his anointing. Because later on God sent a prophet and said that he was rejected although he was still retaining his office. Saul also lost his anointing when he trespassed the office of the priest. This is how he lost his anointing.

In the book of I Samuel 16:14, *Now the Spirit of the LORD departed from Saul, and an evil spirit from the LORD terrorized him.* He lost his anointing but he was still in the office. Why, because the human being still didn't know that he had lost his anointing. And he was still their king. He did not lose his call and his office gift. But he lost the anointing. Sometimes one may lose the anointing but still be in the office for a certain length of time. He remains there due to a grace period while another is chosen to stand in that same office and anointing but is made to wait for God's timetable. Needless to say, the person chosen to fill in that office has to be patient. Remember this if you are not faithful to what God called you to do, God will raise up another. Positions in God's kingdom are not sacred that God has to preserve you no matter what you do. The anointing is precious. You may be called to an office but if you are disobedient, God will remove His anointing first. And after He removed His anointing you can be sure He is going to remove your office.

When the Spirit departed from Saul, God had actually called David and anointed him. Do you know David could have taken over the whole kingdom straightaway? I mean if he could fight Goliath and the bears and the lions, He would have easily defeated Saul in a battle. He was no ordinary man. He grabbed the beard of the lion and he really gave it a good whacking. That's no joke. Do you know why Saul was afraid of him? It is because Saul knows David had the anointing, which he lost. You could lose your anointing and keep your office and that is the most terrible position to be in. Even in this world you have to be qualified in order to hold any office. Even in the natural it works that way. If you are in a company or business,

Deeper Revelations Of The anonting

if you know your work thoroughly and are well qualified, when another new person comes in, you are not threatened. But if another new person comes in and you are not so sure about your work you will feel threatened. Especially if that guy seems to know more than you about the same job that you have suddenly you became a liability. If you still hold a position but have no anointing, you better think about packing your bags. If you have the office and the anointing you know what you will do. Sadly in the body of Christ sometimes positions are retained where the anointing of God has left. When it has left you can be sure it goes to another. And when it goes to another you may become like King Saul.

CHAPTER SIX

DIMENSIONS & DEPTHS IN THE REALM OF THE ANOINTING

What Determines The Level And Depth of Anointing Which A Vessel Can Carry

In A Generation?

Why is it that some ministers are highly anointed than others? What determines the level and depth of anointing which a vessel can carry in a generation? These are some of a myriad of questions which multitudes of believers would ask concerning the appropriation, distribution and administration of the measure of the anointing upon believers. At times people fail to tap into greater dimensions of the anointing because they have a lot of unanswered questions concerning how the anointing operates, why others are more anointed and why others seem to be demonstrating greater dimensions of signs and wonders than the rest. Hence, this revelation is an attempt to provide accurate answers so that believers across the globe can tap into deeper realms of the anointing. However it must be expressly understood that although we have received the same Spirit, our measure of anointing upon us can never be the same in the same way electric gargets don't carry the same measure of electricity in them. This is highly attributable to differences in conductivity levels, degree of consecration, sensitivity to the sprit realm, level of revelation and other divergent reasons.

Unknown to many people, the greatest obstacle that hinders believers from taping and moving in greater depths, higher realms and deeper dimensions of the anointing is a syndrome which I call *celebrating the anointing*. Many people tend to celebrate the anointing that is upon the highly anointed man of God as they watch the spectacular display of the anointing, the glory, glamour and fame that comes with the anointing. The sad thing is that in the process of celebration, they hardly bother or have an interest to get to know how they can get the same anointing for themselves, just like the sons of prophets who were celebrating the anointing that was upon Elijah but never bothered to receive from him. Such a scenario can culminate in a situation whereby some believers have remained at the same bus stop of celebration while others have moved forward to grow and develop their anointing just like Elisha who pursued the anointing upon Elijah until he got a double portion and he instantly became the leader of prophets and moved in greater dimensions of signs and wonders more than ever before. This is the major reason for the differences in measures of the anointing amongst different men of God.

It can be observed that sometimes some ministries are more anointed than others. Elisha and Elijah stood in the same office of a prophet but Elisha was more anointed that Elijah (1 Kings 19:16; 2 Kings 2:9). David and Saul stood in the same office of king but David was more anointed than Saul (1 Samuel 10:1; 16:3). Seven deacons were chosen but Stephen and Philip demonstrated more anointing than the rest (Acts 6:5, 8; 8:5). The question in many people's minds is whether the difference in the levels of anointing was merely the sovereign Will of God or whether there were spiritual principles adhered to that brought the increase in anointing. The answer is both. God's sovereign Will is involved through spiritual principles that He has set in His Word. The following are factors which determine or affect the level of the anointing upon a human vessel.

The will of God manifested through grace:

It is a divine truth that the anointing is given by grace. The Bible says *no man can receive anything unless it is given from above* (John 3:27). This implies that you operate the anointing according to the grace which God has given you. There are different degrees, depths and measures of the anointing that is given by the Holy Spirit through the will of God. The anointing functions according to the will of God as the Spirit wills. It depends on the will of God whether God wants to manifest supernaturally at that moment in time or not. If there is no need for the anointing to manifest, then the anointing will not manifest. The anointing comes when there is a need for it. It depends on the will of God to manifest the anointing although the fullest potential is available.

It is a typical scenario in the church therefore to find vessels carrying different measures of the anointing. By grace, others are highly anointed, other moderately anointed while others are just anointed. Others operate at the ankle deep level, others at knee deep level, some at waist deep level while other carry the dimension of the overflow or measureless anointing. Under such circumstances, in the absence of sacrifices which people make to receive the anointing, it is the law of grace which regulates the appropriation of the anointing through the Holy Ghost.

In view of the above mentioned law of grace which supersedes all spiritual laws, even if one is highly anointed and operates under an overflow anointing, it still has to function according to the will of God. It does not necessarily mean that you will automatically operate that dimension of the anointing in whatever manner you deem necessary. It must be emphasised in this regard that God is not a God of lawlessness, He governs the universe by spiritual laws and principles which we have to tap into. Even the anointing itself is regulated, monitored and administered by the Holy Ghost. Hence, according to spiritual laws governing the flow of the anointing, the anointing upon does not operate all the time, twentyfour hours a day. Instead, it weans and then lifted off you when it is not functional in your life. This implies that even if one has a measureless anointing, it still depends on the will of God, whether God wants you to operate the anointing at that type of meeting or not. If there is no need for the anointing to manifest, then the anointing will not manifest no matter how hard you push it. The anointing comes when there is a need for it. It depends on the will of God to manifest the anointing although the fullest potential you could move in is the measure of anointing God has given you. This explains why some ministers have been so frustrated when they tried to move in the anointing and nothing happened. The key is to be highly sensitive to the Holy Ghost so as to know or establish the will of God in every situation to avoid frustration, disappointment or even judgement. Operating in the anointing outside the context of God's will has serious repercussions and far reaching spiritual consequences on one's destiny, such as the shortening of one's life span, affliction with disease as in the case of Katherine Khulman towards the end of her ministry.

The degree of divine revelation a vessel fathoms

The level of revelation which one has can determine the depth of anointing he can move into. Without a revelation, one cannot move in high levels of the anointing, tread on new grounds, explore new things, move into new avenues of the anointing and migrate into the realm of new manifestations. The degree of revelation one has is directly proportional or tantamount to the degree of anointing he can move into. The secret behind Paul moving into the greater depths of power and anointing is by the abundance of the revelations he had (2 Corinthians 12:7). He received the gospel by revelation and was not taught by man. In the realm of the spirit, you can only accomplish or do what is revealed to you. What is not revealed to you remains a mystery, hidden treasure or a secret. If in a meeting or service one catches a revelation that he can anoint the whole church by waving his hands and having the whole congregation fall under the anointing, it's easy for him to move into that realm. If one has a revelation that by the anointing, the dead can be raised, he can easily move into that realm without any difficulty.

The greatest challenge facing believers across the body of Christ is that so many people are zealous to do exploits, shake the world by God's power and move in the depths of the anointing but they do not have a revelation of how they could reach those depths, dimensions and levels. While it is good to have an insatiable desire and appetite for exploits and fireworks in the kingdom, Paul says *zeal without revelation knowledge is dead* (Proverbs 19:2), hence any zeal must be backed up by a revelation. The bible says *in the days when God called Samuel, there was no widespread revelation* (1 Samuel 3:1) to the extent that even when God called Samuel, he could not identify the voice of God. This implies that without a revelation, it is not possible to get to the depths of knowing the fullness of God and what He has made available for us to partake in. However, it must be understood that we have been ushered into a season of revelation. In this season, only those who will catch the revelation of the anointing encapsulated in this book will launch into greater depths of the miraculous than ever before.

The level of calling and office one administers or governs.

It is a divine truth that concerning matters of the spirit, each calling has a different measure of the anointing. The Bible says God has appointed first appointed apostles and prophets (1 Corinthians 12:28) in the church. As evidenced by the church governance in the early church, apostles seem to be given a higher level of anointing, revelation and commands a greater dimension of authority and power because of the level of their calling. Apostles and prophets have an anointing for breakthrough, ministry establishment, trend setting, laying of new foundations, breaking fallow ground and vision bearing which other people might not move into. This does not mean that other ministry graces are less important. The greater truth is that the level of calling upon one's life is what will determine the level of the anointing one can move into.

For example, a person called into the office of a prophet and a teacher will move into the teaching and prophetic anointing while the person who occupies an office of an evangelist will move in the evangelical anointing. Although at times these ministry graces overlap, it is highly imperative that one functions within the context of God's will by sticking to his calling or office. Functioning outside one's calling is tantamount to stepping out of the perfect the will of God into His permissible will. While by His grace, God gives one a grace period to operate within the faculties of His permissible will, there are consequences that result from disobedience. I have heard of anointed men of God who departed to heaven earlier than expected because they stepped outside the will of God and meddled into certain callings and offices which God never called them into. As reiterated in this publication, God's will prevails in all situations, hence it must not be compromised in any way.

The magnitude or size of the divine vision one bears.

The degree of anointing differs according to the size of one's vision. For example a minister entrusted with a global vision or worldwide ministry can command a higher level of the anointing that one with a local church vision. According to the spiritual laws governing the operation of the anointing, all things held constant, a person who has a ministry of 30 people is not supposed to move at the same level of anointing as the one whose ministry consists of 15 000 people. The size of one's vision is what determines the type and level of the anointing one can manifest. There are local, regional, national and global visions and each command a different level of the anointing. The truth is that the broader the vision, the higher the level of the anointing one can tap into. On the basis of this principle, that is why vision bearers who run Global television broadcasted ministries like Pastor Chris Oyakhilome, Benny Hinn, Dr. Cindy Trimm and others, have tapped into the highest level of the anointing than anybody else in the body of Christ because they have been entrusted with a global vision and the minute a vision goes global, it becomes God's vision. This is a spiritual principle.

The secret is that if you want to increase the measure of the anointing in your life, you must enlarge, broaden and capacitate the size of your vision and a greater anointing will come. Peter and Paul moved into higher realms of the anointing more than other apostles because of the size of their vision. Paul was entrusted with the vision to minister the gospel of Jesus to the gentiles in the global territory; hence he carried a deeper dimension of the anointing. Peter was entrusted with the vision to preach to the Jews across the world, hence a greater anointing was imparted upon him for that specific vision.

The Nature of assignment to be executed or accomplished by a vessel:

The level of commission determines the amount of anointing which a vessel can carry. Some people are more anointed than others because of the nature of their assignment. In every generation, God raises people and uses them in special ministries, and visions to usher peculiar spiritual experiences and manifestations and drive generational or dispensational visions. Because of the nature of such special assignments, high levels of anointing are released upon such vessels to accomplish God's work. For example, if the assignment requires that one raises the dead in masses, definitely greater levels of the anointing will be needed to execute such tasks. This is the reason why people like Smith Wigglesworth were highly anointed because God used them in a special assignment of raising the dead. To cement this revelation with reference to scriptural evidence, Peter was highly anointed because God used him a special way for his shadow to bring about mass healing to the sick in his generation. Elijah was used in a special assignment to the extent of shutting and opening the heavens at his own discretion or prerogative and was caught up to the heaven. Elisha was used by God to carry out His special assignments and was given greater anointing, and this is why his bones still retained the anointing to the extent that a dead a man who came into contact with his bones long after he was dead, was raised back to life. Moses was given a special assignment to take the whole nation of Israel out of the land of Egypt and because of the nature of assignment God gave him a special anointing to perform miracles, signs and wonders. Jesus had a special assignment to redeem the whole world by dying on the cross and because of the nature of this assignment, He carried measureless anointing than anybody else. Philip was used by God to carry the gospel of Jesus from Jerusalem to distant places during the time when transportation was a challenge and because of the nature of assignment, he was caught up in the spirit and divinely transported or carried by the tidal waves of the spirit to Azotus.

Several generations down the line, other men and women of God such as John G. Lake, William Brahman, Maria Woodworth-Etter, Kenneth Hagin and Kathrine Khulman were used by God in special assignments, hence they carried excessively high levels of the anointing. The greater truth is that ministers whose ministries are characterised by unique, rare or peculiar manifestations will do more miracles, signs and wonders and mighty deeds just like the apostles. This is because the anointing is given according to the nature of the assignment. That is why there is an anointing for breakthrough, an anointing for wealth or finances, an anointing for dominion, an anointing for miracles, signs and wonders, a prophetic anointing and depending on the nature of the assignment to be done, one is given a corresponding anointing to accomplish it.

The level of faith which a vessel professes or exhibits

It is specified in the scripture that *God has given to every believer a specific measure of faith* (Romans 12:3). While God gives a spirit without measure, the level of faith one commands is what will determine the depth of the anointing he can tap into. It is the force or power of faith that will catapult one to move into higher realms of glory and greater depths into His presence. Faith is a fundamental prerequisite or requirement for one to move in the spirit. Faith is what gives you a legal entrance into the supernatural, hence it is totally unacceptable or illegitimate for one to be seen parading the streets of the spirit world without faith. That is why the Bible says *without faith it is impossible to please God* (Hebrews 11:6) because God lives in the realm of faith and it is through faith that we get to fellowship with Him in the realm of the spirit. Without faith it is impossible to please God and by the same token without faith it is impossible to move in the anointing because it takes a significant level of faith to move in the anointing.

The degree of authority one commands in the spirit realm

The level of anointing which one can manifest is determined by the level of authority which he commands. According the spiritual laws and principles governing the realm of the spirit, the anointing flows through authority. It must be expressly understood that protocol is observed in the realm of the spirit, just like in the natural. Therefore, those who command high levels of authority in the realm of the spirit are likely to move into the depths of the anointing. The demon that possessed the sons of Sceva questioned their authority to move in the spirit because they did not have the anointing. How do I know that? Because it is the anointing that gives one authority. Paul and Jesus had greater anointing and commanded high levels of authority in the spirit but the sons of Sceva were not known in the spirit because they did not have authority and the anointing to operate in that realm.

There is a highest level of authority in the realm of territorial governance we can move into called *dominion*. This is the kind of power which God originally gave to Adam. Through this God-given mandated authority, Adam was able to call and name animals and operate as a spirit being. After the fall of man, that authority was lost but by reason of the death and resurrection of Jesus Christ from the dead, that authority has been bestowed upon us. By this authority, we can re-arrange things in the spirit, shift tables, change situations and circumstances, re-create the world around us and enlarge our sphere of influence and determine at our discretion, the kind of world we want to live in. When the Bible says *we shall declare a thing and it shall be established for us* (Job 22:28), it actually speaks of the operation of this God given authority or dominion.

The greater truth is that greater measures of the anointing flows through this kind of authority. It is the same kind of authority by which God created the world and commanded light to appear and it was so. People who have mastered territorial dominion and subdued territories are likely to move in that greater dimension of the anointing. The spiritual covering that comes upon an individual to exercise the kind of authority or dominion over a territory is called a *mantle*. Mantles fall upon those who move in the realm of territorial dominion and is given to enable individuals to govern, rule, reign, enforce, subdue, conquer, enthrone territories in the realm of the spirit on behalf of the kingdom.

The level of desire, hunger, thirst or appetite one manifest move in the anointing

It is important to unveil the divine truth that having a spiritual desire is such a powerful force such that it can draw or provoke the supernatural to manifest instantaneously in the natural. When Peter came to minister, his kin folks, the hunger and expectation level was so high that before Peter could finish his sermon, the rain of the anointing poured upon them (Acts 10:44). The Bible says *as Peter began to speak, the Holy Ghost instantly fell upon all those who heard the word*. While we might be tempted to think that it is because Peter was highly anointed that he moved in that dimension of the anointing, the greater truth is that there was a high expectancy level from the congregation as they had developed an insatiable appetite and perennial hunger for the supernatural. Spiritual hunger is an important ingredient in drawing upon the anointing. Elisha demonstrated a deeper hunger for the anointing upon Elijah for a long time. He persistently followed Elijah through Gilgal, Bethel, Jericho and the Jordan River (2 Kings 1-6). Notice how Elijah seemingly wanted to shake this persistent Elisha off by asking him to stay while he went on. However, Elisha was like a bulldog who had seen the power of the anointing on Elijah and was so hungry for it that he would not let him go until he received a double portion of it. At the end, Elisha was rewarded for spiritual hunger and persistence.

To substantiate this revelation with further scriptural evidence, Jacob desired the blessing to the extent of wrestling with an angel and breaking his hip because he desperately needed a blessing from God. Unless you are desperate for the power, anointing or the miraculous, you might not fully partake of greater volumes of the anointing because the realm of the miraculous is provoked by desire. *Therefore the extent to which you may receive the anointing from God is determined by how hungry or thirsty you are for the miraculous.* It is therefore advisable that you develop an insatiable appetite for the supernatural in order to receive an avalanche of God's power.

By operation, the anointing flows or runs like a tap of water. If you open the tap, water runs down if you close it stops. In a like manner, if you hunger for the anointing and you open your spirit or you are rightly positioned in the spirit to receive, then you can provoke or trigger the flow of the anointing. The things of God are received through hunger and desire. This is a spiritual principle. *By this principle, there is an open invitation for men in the furthest extremes of the world, to partake of the anointing.* Jesus said, "*If anyone is thirst let him come and drink*". This does not speak of physical drinking but the taking in of the substance *the anointing*. This implies that the anointing automatically comes by thirst, hunger and longing. Elisha got a double portion of the anointing through this principle. Jesus said *anyone who believes in me shall rivers of living water flow from within him* (John 7:38) and by this He spoke of the anointing.

The Extent to which the human spirit is developed or the degree of openness of the human spirit

Deeper Revelations Of The anonting

The extent to which one's spirit is opened determines how much of the anointing can flow into him. The more open the vessel is to the anointing, the more volumes of the anointing are likely to come upon him just like an open tap of water releases more gallons of water. The extent to which the spirit of a man is opened is such a critical determinant to the receptivity of the anointing because God uses the human spirit to touch the congregation. On the other hand, if it is closed, God is not able to fully use it but if it is rightly positioned in the spirit to receive, then more is imparted upon it. The size of the human spirit will determine the amount of anointing it can carry. The human spirit is developed as we fellowship with the Holy Ghost and spend time in the presence, make sacrifices through prayer and fasting as well as through meditation. The early church prayed together and God released an anointing on them so powerfully that the house they were in was shaken (Acts 4:31). The extent of the development of their inner man as well as an increased level of anointing upon their lives produced a greater manifestation of power (Acts 4:33). This is the reason why it is a common experience in various ministries that it is easier to minister to a prayerful group than a prayerless one. The anointing flows more easily in a prayer full group than a prayerless one.

In Romans 1:9, Paul contends *that he serves God with his spirit*. At this level, our spirit becomes the vehicle by which the Holy Spirit uses in order to flow and bless mankind. In a ministerial context, our spirit is not put aside and the Spirit just bypasses you. No! The Spirit has to pass systematically as the ark of glory in your spirit man and He has to flow through your soul and He has to flow through your body. Therefore, how great God can truly use you depends to a certain extent on the development of your spirit man, the renewal of your mind and the consecration of your body. Now each one has yielded in different proportions in different areas. Some people want to yield everything but their spirits are under developed. Some are almost half dead. Their spirit has not been fed for a long time. So we need to develop our spirit man in order for our spirit man to receive the impressions of the spirit world. And the stronger you develop your spirit man, the more the Holy Spirit can use you. And that takes meditation on the word and many other keys to develop it. *Moreover, the extent to which your spirit is cultivated through deep and incessant worship will determine how much anointing will flow into your life*. Worship is a magnet for the Holy Spirit. We need the spirit of worship upon our lives. This will cause the Holy Spirit water level to rise within us. Worship will open up your heart to receive more volumes of the anointing on your life.

The nature and type of meeting that you are conducting

At times the level of anointing which one could flow into or operate depends on the type of the meeting. For example, prophetic meetings or services would naturally require one to move in the prophetic anointing, healing meetings will require one to move on the healing anointing. An evangelist who is highly anointed and who does not function in the office of a prophet might not move deeper in a prophetic meeting that requires taping into the prophetic unction even if he is anointed. This is one of the *limitations of the anointing*. At times the anointing comes in a meeting but does not flow that much, not because the minister is not anointed but because of the nature of the meeting.

The reality is that you can only move into the depths, dimension and grace which the Lord has called you into, although these ministerial graces at times overlap. This is why Peter said, *"Silver and gold have I none but such as I have, give I thee in the name of Jesus rise up and walk"*. In other words, Peter knew the exact grace and ministry which the Lord has given him i.e that of manifesting healing through signs and wonders. At that point in time, Peter did not have the *prophetic anointing* upon him to prophesy regarding the condition of the man. Instead, he had the *healing anointing* which he was capacitated to release upon the man. Just like Peter we need to know what we have and what we do not have and this will help us to move in the graces and dimensions of the anointing God has given us.

The expectancy level of the people being ministered to

The expectancy level that people have of you can determine the level of anointing which can operate through you. People need to maintain a level of expectancy from the minister of God because it is the expectancy level that will determine the amount of blessings people will receive from God. It is a typical scenario in the Christian faith that some people just attend meetings for the sake of registering their presence and without expecting to receive any anointing or blessings and unknown to them such a tendency has a negative bearing on how the anointing moves. If the expectancy level in the congregation is very high, a minister could operate at a higher level. This is a spiritual principle. For example, if a highly anointed minister goes to a meeting where everybody did not expect or really look forward to him operating in that anointing, he might not function to his full potential. This is because the people did not pay a price to be ministered by him. That is why Paul said brethren *I longed to see you so that I could impart a spiritual gift* (Romans 1:11) and he continues to mention that *though I wanted to come, I have been hindered so that when I come I might have some fruits amongst you.* In other words, although he was ready and wanted to visit the brethren, their expectancy level of him was low, hence Paul postponed his visit till their expectancy level was well cultivated enough for them to receive from him. This implies that where the expectancy level is high, impartation is made easier. The truth is that there is a price that people pay to be ministered to, for example, some people will travel land, sea, and air to get ministered by you. On the contrary, some people just live next door to the church and say, *"If I like it, I will be there. If I do not like it, I will not be there."* Hence, the level of expectancy is low. For expectancy, people need to pay a price. If they do not pay a price, they do not have expectancy. When they pay a price, they have expectancy. Just like the minister needs to prepare himself, the people also need to prepare themselves before a meeting.

The other reason why sometimes the anointing works powerfully in some ministers' lives is because they build people's expectancy of them. They are not so accessible, but show up only when it is time to minister and when ministering is ended, one goes off. In other words, they make a grand entrance and secretly exit the meetings. There is a psychological factor being placed on the minister as people do not have easy access to the man of God. As a result, they look up to that person and have higher expectations of him, you put them on a higher level and your expectancy level goes up. Stirring up or provoking the crowd by practically demonstrating the power of God at the beginning of a ministerial session can make the crowd to have a high expectancy level during the service.

The truth is that when people are expectant, there is the potential to operate at a higher level. Jesus could do no mighty works in His own city, because the people there did not receive Him. They were offended at Him and that stopped the flow of God's anointing (Matthew 13:58). However, many people were healed when the expectancy was high and the power of God was present to heal them (Luke 5:17). Some people pay a high price to receive their miracle. They may have to push through the crowd like the woman with the issue of blood (Matthew 5:25) or they may have to shout to draw attention to their plight (Matthew 20:30). Some may have travelled long distances with the hope of receiving.

Frequency Revelator

The level of your own preparedness as a minister

The degree of your preparedness as a minister determines the level of anointing that will flow through you during ministerial session. Sometimes you may not be more prepared than the other times. Sometimes you may be able to spend time waiting on God more than other times. During that time, you have spent more time waiting on God. In your preparedness, you are more able to tap into the full measure of the anointing on your life. If you have done all the necessary preparation that you could for a meeting and if you are a ten volts anointed minister, you will flow at the level of ten volts subject to the other third reason. You have these ten volts in your life. Sometimes maybe during the day you are running about and doing too many things. Perhaps you have an evangelistic meeting in London. You few all the way there. You had a good rest and the meeting is the next night. In the morning of the next day, you go all over London sightseeing. In the afternoon, you had a large helping of the English delicacies for lunch. Then you go and do all your shopping. Just about an hour before the meeting, you rush back into your hotel. You washed yourself quickly and go to the meeting. You may have ten volts but you may be able to flow only in about five volts of anointing since you have lowered your preparedness. You did not shut yourself aside to consecrate yourself to the Lord.

We should realize that preparedness is necessary. By preparedness, I mean your personal relationship with God. There is a degree of preparedness. When I travel to places, I hardly go sightseeing. The only time I could do so is when the meeting is over. Preparedness affects the anointing of God in our life. If God calls you to minister in some way, God will expect you to fully give yourself. That is what we mean by giving yourself to your office and ministry. For that reason, Jesus in John 17 says *for this purpose, I sanctify Myself*. He consecrated Himself because He has such a high mission for us. He gave Himself entirely to the Lord.

The level of the anointing will vary according to a believer's preparedness. Sometimes, Christians are more prepared than at other times. Sometimes they may be able to spend time waiting on God more than other times. It is important to spend time in fellowship and intimacy with God in order to build up a preparedness to move when the Spirit moves. By being prepared, Christians are more able to tap into the full measure of the anointing upon their life. There is a price to pay in anointed ministry, such as waiting upon the Lord, praying, fasting, studying the Word and seeking the mind of the Spirit. There are sacrifices that have to be made in order to walk in God's fullness. Preparedness affects the anointing of God upon an individual's life. When God places a call upon a person, he expects total submission. This almost always means turning off the voice of the flesh. Jesus said that He sanctified Himself for the purpose of anointed ministry (John 17). He consecrated Himself because He had such a high mission for the sheep. He gave Himself entirely to the Lord.

The level of sensitivity and Obedience to the voice of the Holy Spirit

The major problem in the church today is that Christians are not listening to God. They are doing their own thing. If you ever want to see the anointing of the Holy Spirit, you must listen to the Holy Spirit. Firstly, you must have the anointing of the Holy Spirit. Secondly, you must wait for His instructions and directions. You cannot do as you wish. If you persist in ignoring the Holy Spirit's instruction, you will be taken out of ministry. Finally, when you obey the Holy Spirit, there will be a manifestation. The Holy Spirit will bear witness to you. The Holy Spirit is showing us these types of anointing to prepare us for the end times.

We need to value to Presence of the Holy Spirit in our lives to walk in His anointing. We are told not to "grieve" the Holy Spirit. Most people would not know the Holy Spirit has left because He has been gone so long. There is a place of being aware of the Holy Spirit's presence in our lives. It is when this tangible awareness is with us that we can actually tell that He is grieved by certain things. To be grieved means to be upset or unhappy. We want God to be happy within us. The Holy Spirit is God within us. We are habitations of God. God dwells in us in the person of the Holy Spirit. Of all the principles in ministry that we learn, including all the training that Bible Colleges and Theological Seminaries can offer, the most important preparation for the ministry is to get to know the person of the Holy Spirit. Anyone who learns to relate to the person of the Holy Spirit intimately will be a success everywhere and every time. He is the key behind all keys. The Minister behind all ministers. He is the unseen, sometimes unknown, many times unwelcomed person behind the church scene. It is a sad fact that in much of the training of ministers, there is virtually little or no training to get acquainted with the lovely person of the Holy Spirit.

It is evident that the Holy Spirit was a real person to the early church and not just an unknown force. He was a real person who spoke and instructed.

He bears witness together with us (John 15:26, 27). Peter, standing before the Sanhedrin, declared that the Holy Spirit was his witness (Acts 5:32). If we really desire the release of the Holy Spirit's power through our lives, then we have to learn to relate to the Holy Spirit as a person. It is the power of God that makes the difference (1 Corinthians 4:19, 20). God's power does not solely depend upon Moses, Elijah, Elisha, Paul,

Peter or Stephen or any other biblical character. It depends upon the PERSON of the Holy Spirit working through yielded vessels. Jesus, our lord and Saviour, Himself, yielded to the Holy Spirit fully. Jesus did not start His ministry until the Holy Spirit had come upon Him. But when He was anointed with the Holy Spirit, He did in three years all that He wanted to do and with great power (Acts 10:38

CHAPTER SEVEN

DIVINE PRINCIPLES OF OPERATING IN THE REALM OF ANOINTING

There are three main keys to operating in the anointing. The first key is to discern the purpose and type of anointing manifesting. The third key is to receive the manifestation of the anointing. The second is to learn how to channel the manifested anointing. However, there are other divergent keys that we can use to unlock the supernatural realm and release the rain of the anointing in a greater measure. Any man of God who seem to be moving in deeper dimensions of the anointing is because he has learnt the art of tapping into these principles. There is a difference between being anointed and being able to propagate the anointing. Some man of God are anointed by their anointing is not seen because they have not learnt the principles of how to channel it, direct it and cause it to rain upon the masses. The following are therefore keys that can unlock the treasure of the anointing in your spirit and catapult you to greater dimensions of the anointing you have never dreamed possible.

RELEASING THE ANOINTING

A lot of believers have the believer's anointing but they don't know how to release it. The only way to keep the anointing is to give it away. The anointing can be released through *faith* and *confession*. Therefore, one of the key laws of operating in the believer's anointing is to understand the power of words. Words are the capsules that contain the believer's anointing and release it forth. The believer's anointing in all five realms depends on the word we speak. The next time you want to release the believer's anointing over anything, speak it out verbally. That is why we say grace over food. You know we are releasing tremendous authority and power over substances that you partake of. When you make a confession over your home, you are releasing the anointing, and this anointing is not the anointing upon but the anointing within. Words are powerful and believers are not using them enough. You are not taking authority. Exousia is not operating. Believers are just as dumb as Adam standing next to the woman letting her talk to the serpent. David was a man of war. However, we see that his life was marked with a tremendous outflow of worship and psalms. Remember, we said that where there is an *inflow* there is an *outflow*. Unless we release the outflow, there is no further inflow of the anointing into our life. Whenever the anointing comes upon David's life, he would always sing or speak forth God's praises in songs and psalms. This is the essence of releasing the anointing. He expressed himself in worship unto God. There is an outflow from his life. There could be many types of outflow in different lives or even in the same life, there could be many types of outflow but some outflows would feature more prominently than others. In David's life, the outflow of the psalms and worship stands out strongly. He is known as a sweet psalmist of Israel. In other people's lives, the outflow may be strongly manifested in other areas. In some people's lives, the outflow is shaking. They may not be that good in singing and worshiping. That is not their field. When the anointing comes into their life, they get into a shaking. I am not saying that the Holy Spirit causes all types of manifestations. There could be demonic imitation or it could be just simply the flesh. However, that does not rule out the fact that there are genuine ones. The problem is not whether there is a manifestation or not. It is a matter of discerning the type and origin of the manifestations. A manifestation of shaking comes on some people. For some people, the anointing is manifested through prophesying. Some people would just rock to and fro when the anointing of God comes upon their life. When the tangible anointing of God in a person's life is released, demons can sense it very much because they are creatures in the spirit world. Demons know what spiritual substance is. Human being tends to live more on the flesh and be more conscious of the flesh area. Demons are very sensitive to the spirit world because they themselves are spirit beings. So when you take the anointing and put on some person who is attacked by demon, the demon feels it even more that that person.

Some people only moved into level one. At level one, we learn to recognize how it comes. At level two, we learn when it is not there how to bring it about. We need to know how to discover your particular way of bringing down the anointing. How do we discover the way in which the anointing can come in our life? By examining your particular manifestation when you first receive the anointing. When you first received the anointing and you prophesy you can be assured that you keep on prophesying to maintain it. If the anointing came upon you and your hand shakes, the next time you want the anointing of God, wait on Him, get into the atmosphere you learn and you stir and you sense that little handshake coming. Now, this kind of stirring is a little bit like Samson. Let us look at Samson as he operates in the anointing. In the book of Judges, Samson has a particular way of moving in the anointing and his anointing was tremendous. He had such a powerful

Deeper Revelations Of The anonting

strength that came supernaturally. I want to point to you the fact that when his head was shaved and his covenant was broken, the anointing was lifted up from him. In Judges 16, a phrase there gives you an incident that could point to how he did it in verse 20. And she said, *"The Philistines are upon you, Samson!"* Therefore, he awoke from his sleep, and said, *"I will go out as before, at other times, and shake myself free!"* But he did not know that the Lord had departed from him. When Samson had the anointing come upon his life, he seems to have this shaking. When he wants the anointing, he seems to get it. Let me point to some local kind of situation that you could identify it with. There is a sense where you know that the anointing is bubbling forth you just have to release it for it to come forth. In any meeting or in any situation where you know that the anointing is hovering and ready to be released, you know exactly when it will be released. You could sense it. You could withhold it also. On the other hand, you could release more of it when you learn how the anointing comes on your life and what its side effects are.

What other ways could it be experienced? Some people may not experience that kind of warmth. They may experience it differently. They may experience a kind of cold wind blowing. It does not mean that it always has to be hot. Some people say that since God is hot, then cold sensation is from the devil. Hell is hot too. We cannot use that as a theology. For whatever reason sometimes when people sense the anointing they feel this cold shower over them. It comes in waves. Therefore, they have to learn to recognize when it comes, how it comes. If you observe Kathryn Kuhlman very carefully, she always lifts up her hands. Some people would need to lift up their hands before they get it. For example, in your first experience, you sensed the bubbling of the anointing of God and found that the anointing was released when you just lifted up your hands. Then the next time you sense the bubbling, you release it by lifting up your hands again, and the same anointing comes. Your particular anointing is released through what I call a release of faith God has given to you. It is just as if God has given you a teaching anointing you would have the confidence to operate in it even though at that time you are invited you don't have the anointing upon you. Let's say suddenly you are called to teach. You could depend on that teaching anointing to bring forth the Word through your life. You could allow it to have demands made on the anointing and developed a confidence in the gift of God in your life.

In this level two is that not only do we learn how to stir it, the way we learn to stir it is to recognize the peculiarity of how it first outflow through our life. When the first outflow of the anointing happened when you praised and worshipped God, or when you lifted up your hands, or playing your guitar, maintain what you did. Remember in all these outward manifestations, it is assumed that your relationship with God is fine. If your relationship with God is not fine, you will be like Samson, thinking that since you have been moving in the anointing regularly by a particular release of faith, it will come automatically. However, if you have left the Holy Spirit, and you tried to release the anointing by your usual release of faith, nothing will happen. When you know there is a peculiar way in which it always comes, you could rely on it as long as your relationship with the Holy Spirit is right. You could rely on it as surely as you rely on a weapon in your life, which you have learned to use. You could definitely rely on that when you learned to operate in that and you know the anointing is on that. When your relationship is not right and you try to rely on that, you will be like Samson. You go through all the motions, the right actions, but if you have no relationship with the Holy Spirit, nothing comes forth but the flesh. It works if you have a relationship with the Holy Spirit but it does not work if you do not have a relationship with the Holy Spirit. It wasn't just the mantle—the hairy coat—that divided the waters; if it had been, everyone could have parted waters, because they all wore skin coats—*it was the anointing that did it.* That's why the sons of the prophets said, *"The spirit of Elijah does rest on Elisha."*

In this very hour in which we are living, the Lord is releasing His anointing on His people to a degree unseen since the first century. He wants to not only anoint us, but He wants to teach us how to steward it, how to release it, and how to increase it in our lives. He wants to give us spiritual victory. It is critically important that we be alert and ready to step into this season of divine appointment. God is calling us to welcome His anointing and take our places in the most glorious hour of the Church. God is imparting His anointing to us for our own healing and deliverance, but there is more. He wants us to be so empowered and energized with His anointing that we become instruments of His miracles for others. It is the anointing that breaks the yoke. We are coming into a new prophetic hour, and God is calling us to become carriers of His glory that will break the yokes of bondage, sin and sickness and set His people free wherever we go. A key to walking in and releasing the anointing is love. Everything Jesus did was motivated by His compassion: *"But when He saw the multitudes, He was moved with compassion for them"* (Matthew 9:36). In the same way, anyone who carries the healing anointing must also carry a heart consumed with compassion for those in need. The spirits of pride, criticism, condemnation, prejudice, legalism and judgmentalism are completely incompatible with the anointing of the Spirit.

In order to do the works of Jesus, we must be *like* Jesus. The only way to be like Jesus is to let Him live His resurrection life in us.

Deeper Revelations Of The anonting

RECOGNITION OR ACKNOWLEDGEMENT OF THE ANOINTING

There is an anointing on you, whether you recognize it or not, if you're called to any office or ministry. No matter which office you stand in, or what you are called to do, you can have something to do with determining the *degree of* your anointing. You can prepare yourself for this anointing. If it doesn't come on you, it's because you didn't prepare yourself. Therefore, we all must recognize the anointing coming in our life. You must know when it comes. Recognize the sensation; recognize the tangibility, and how it comes to your life. God is not against us analysing this thing. Therefore, we need to recognize how it comes into our life. If every time the anointing comes upon you and your hands feel like shaking, you know the anointing is there for you. There is another sub-law that we bring into this. Our experience of the Lord can change as we grow in the Lord. You must add in that factor. Once we learn to recognize His manifestation and how it comes, be aware of this sub-point, as we grow in Him and walk with Him through the years, His manifestation in our life can change. In other words, He may not exactly manifest the anointing like He did to you two or three years ago. You will know the change as it comes. Usually the change comes at each phase.

There are different phases in the graduation of the anointing. Usually when we move from one phase to the next phase, the sensation changes. You experience changes in the anointing upon your life when you enter a new phase in your life and ministry. You know that it is a different phase and a different anointing of God that you are moving in. We keep growing from glory to glory, phase to phase in a different anointing of God. You must not forget this sub-clause. Otherwise, you may keep looking for the old manifestation and familiar anointing when God is bringing you to a new phase and new working in your life. Why is it that way? There are so many varied manifestations of the anointing, each of them having a different effect on our life. If you understand the peculiarities and the specific tangibility of the anointing in your life and you know that it's God not the flesh, do not try to do it when you are still in the flesh and no anointing has descended upon you yet. When you know that is God, it becomes your way of knowing when the anointing has come.

PERCEIVING THE ANOINTING OR DISCERNING THE ANOINTING

To have a manifestation of the anointing is to tangibly perceive the anointing. We need to perceive the anointing , when it is there and when it is not, then a lot of spiritual progress is going to be made by the Church. Like Elisha, unless we know the Spirit has come upon us, we could not operate our spiritual offices (2 Kings 3). The tangibility of the anointing can be sensed in different ways by different individuals. There are varieties of operations (1 Corinthians 12:6). Whatever the method or way of sensing, we must discern the manifestation when it comes. If we are not able to receive the first key of having the anointing manifested in our lives, we should spend our time meditating on the Word of God (*not just reading*), worshipping God in tongues and with the understanding, and praying many hours in tongues. Praying in tongues energizes us to a level where we can easily sense the anointing. Once we have a manifestation of the anointing we can familiarize ourselves with it, making it easier and easier to sense the anointing. It would also take a shorter time to receive the anointing from thenceforth.

Therefore, it is imperative to discern the purpose or type of anointing manifesting. There are many types of anointing and each produces a different work. The healing anointing cannot be used for teaching and vice versa. The anointing to get people baptized in the Spirit cannot be used for healing. There are as many anointings as there are of the types of work of the Holy Spirit. Some types of anointing manifest the side effect of falling under the power. However, in the teaching anointing (*the Spirit of wisdom and revelation*), there is no sense in people falling because they need to consciously hear and understand as well as refer to their Bibles. When manifesting the anointing to get people baptized with the Holy Spirit, it is more important to have them speak with tongues than to have them fall under the power. It is alright if they fall and speak in tongues at the same time but many times I have observed that those ministering are satisfied when they fall, without helping them into the realm of tongues. The sign of receiving the baptism in the Holy Spirit is speaking in tongues and not falling under the power.

Other people might perceive the anointing only through a warm sensation in my heart. I felt like Luke 24 when Jesus was walking with the two disciples on the way to Emmaus. After Jesus disappeared and when they realized it was Jesus, they said to one another, *"Did not our hearts warm when He spoke?"* I felt that sensation. After that, the anointing began to operate a little bit differently, where I not only sense warmth over my heart area, I sensed a warmth all over my head. Therefore, it increased. Together with that, I get a few other peculiar signals for different types of sicknesses, diseases, and problems. I learn to recognize the peculiarity of these manifestations. I moved into that for some time. Later on, the Lord changed it again and now I feel warmth from the top of my head to the tip of my toes. When the anointing for revelation comes, I sense it flow at the centre of my head. When the prophetic anointing comes upon me, I feel it as a sensation in my heart area and when the anointing for signs and wonders comes, my right hand shakes vehemently. For Kenneth Hagin, the anointing is like a coat thrown over him. Each person has a peculiar way of experiencing it. However, peculiar and particular you must learn to recognize the anointing of God in your life. How does it come and what does it do? That is the first area, recognize your individual peculiarity of your anointing and once you have mastered that, tapping into greater dimensions of the anointing for signs and wonders will be like a stroll through a park.

ACTIVATING THE ANOINTING

It is worth exploring the divine truth that the anointing requires activation for it to function in its full capacity. Smith Wigglesworth once said in his book. *"When the Holy Ghost does not move, I move the Holy Ghost"*. That is a very strange statement to say. When you take that statement out of context, it can give rise to dangerous ideas. The Holy Spirit is God, and we cannot arm-twist Him to do our bidding. However, Smith Wigglesworth is saying that he has learned to recognize how the Holy Spirit moves. He knows like Elisha how to get into the anointing when he has a need. He knows how to move into the anointing when he needs it. That is where we say we need to understand our own peculiar sensation and know how to stir the anointing. Therefore, one of the most valuable lessons to learn in Christ is to stir it up inside of you. Each of us are anointed differently. One thing is clear it is the anointing (*or the empowerment of the Holy Spirit*) that defeats the enemy (Isaiah 10:27): *And it shall come to pass in that day, that his burden shall be taken away from off thy shoulder, and his yoke from off thy neck and the yoke shall be destroyed because of the anointing.* A yoke is a heavy band tied upon the shoulders typically binding two oxen together to force them to use their strength to labour for that person guiding them.

The anointing upon does not remain permanently on our life. When the work is over that it has come to perform the anointing is lifted off. There are times where there is a demand made on the anointing and when it is not there we need to learn to stir it forth. Elisha had firstly learned to recognize his individual peculiarity of his anointing and secondly, he also learned how to get the anointing when it was not there. He learned how to stir up what was called to be upon his life and what was rightfully his to function in. He learned to stir it up. He purposely asked for a musician. While the musician played, it must have helped him to get into a certain stage where he could move into the anointing of God. David was a psalmist. In the anointing upon, (*we are not talking about the anointing within*) the anointing upon comes and goes as the Spirit wills. The anointing upon does not remain permanently on our life. When the work is over that it has come to perform, the anointing is lifted off. There are times where there is a demand made on the anointing and when it is not there we need to learn to stir it forth. Elisha learnt how to stir it up and likewise, David learnt the same. Suppose David wanted to draw on a greater measure of the anointing, I know the first thing that he would do. He would take his harp and play it until the anointing comes upon him. Music plays a big role in the anointing upon. If you watch Kathryn Kuhlman's videotapes, you will find that music played a big role in her moving into the anointing upon her life. Kenneth E. Hagin has also mentioned that. You could be ministering under the anointing upon but if suddenly the musicians play the wrong music, the Holy Spirit is grieved and the anointing is lifted up. There is an anointing upon that we learn to recognize. David learnt to get it by music.

Carefully consider the following prophetic instruction which Samuel gave Saul in I Samuel 10:5: *After that you shall come to the hill of God where the Philistine garrison is. And it will happen, when you have come there to the city, that you will meet a group of prophets coming down from the high place with a stringed instrument, a tambourine, a flute, and a harp before them and they will be prophesying.* Notice the phrase *"they will be prophesying."* Now, this is a group of prophets. They were stirring the anointing upon their life through music. The anointing was definitely upon them. As Saul passed by, the anointing that was upon their life jumped off them and came on Saul. There was an anointing upon. The question is: Why they were doing what they were doing? They were activating the anointing. Why won't this group of prophets sit cross-legged under the terebinth tree waiting on God? It was not their way to stir up the anointing of God. The way that they had discovered for their lives was to constantly play music. It stirs the anointing on their life. They had reached level two.

For clarity of purpose, let us refer to another complementary scripture in 2 Kings Chapter 3, whereby Elisha was asked to prophesy because the three Kings had problems. Then Elisha said to the king of Israel, *"What have I to do with you? Go to the prophets of your father and the prophets of your mother."* But the king of Israel said to him, *"No, for the Lord has called these three kings together to deliver them into the hand of Moab."* And Elisha said, *"As the Lord of hosts lives, before whom I stand, surely were it not that I regard the presence of Jehoshaphat king of Judah, I would not look at you, nor see you. But bring me a musician." Then it happened, when the musician played, that the hand of the Lord came upon him. And he said thus says the Lord.* It is scripturally evident that Elisha recognized the anointing coming on him. Before that, he recognized that it was not there. I can observe that Elisha knew what the anointing was like in his own life. He knew it when it came. He knew it when it was not there. He must have some way of knowing. Therefore, he has reached that first point where he learnt to recognize the peculiarity of his own anointing. That takes experimentation.

Deeper Revelations Of The anonting

These things that we teach you got to put into practice the next time that you move into the anointing. Sometimes when you start and you are not sure but you examine it after everything is over to see how the anointing was. To see whether there was really an anointing, check the result. See the anointing produces results.

CHANNELLING THE ANOINTING

Once we have discerned the type of anointing, we have to discern how to channel it. Channelling the anointing means directing it or flowing in the direction in which the Holy Spirit wants the anointing to move. Whenever the anointing comes upon a place, it fills the atmosphere but we must know how to place a demand or make a pulling on that mantle so that we can move in a specific direction to give birth to supernatural manifestations in the natural realm. For example, if a healing anointing is present, we would have to listen carefully to the Holy Spirit whether He wants us to lay hands on them, use oil, have them lay hands on themselves, have them stand in a row and blow on them or use handkerchiefs. There are always many, many ways to channel the same anointing. Channelling is a release of faith and anointing at the same time. Notice that Jesus uses a variety of methods to channel the healing anointing: by the spoken word, by using clay, by spitting or by touch. Jesus was sensitive to the Holy Spirit and did not patent a method. Many preachers are not sensitive to the Holy Spirit on this third key. They are satisfied with the first two and get stereotyped on one method for channelling the anointing. The methods of channelling the anointing are determined by the specific instructions of the Holy Spirit on each occasion, by the level of anointing manifesting and by God's personal instruction to the minister to operate a method. God sometimes requires certain individuals to use a particular method e.g. Moses using the rod – Exodus 4:17, believers laying hands – Mark 16:18, elders anointing with oil – James 5:14). The best approach in this third key is to keep an open ear to the Holy Spirit even when we have discerned the manifested anointing.

Why does the demon come out when handkerchiefs were laid on the sick? They must have felt something. They did not hear any command. They did not hear any voice. Whether they were hanging inside or outside the person's soul or body, the moment the handkerchief came and touched that person, the demons would feel the force that pushes them away. Some thing would expel them. There was some force that prevents them from hanging on to that body. It was the anointing of God being channelled for a purpose and for a reason. The anointing of God can be channelled. In other words when the anointing is there, you can just leave it there and nothing will happen. You need to take the anointing of God and channel it. Electricity was in the air ever since this world was made. But it has only been in the 20th century that man has been able to tap on the power of electricity that was in the air all along. As long as the anointing of God is in the air, we can draw it in and channel it to perform a task. We can channel it to perform deliverance. We can channel it to do anything. And it is a tangible force that is there. That is the anointing of God. A tangible force was there. When the woman with the issue of blood touched Jesus, Jesus felt something flowing out. No word was spoken or anything. In fact Jesus was on the way to Jairus' house. There was a release at that point and the anointing goes. So there is a point of release. When you reach a person before the point of release there wouldn't be any flow of the anointing of God.

The level of anointing manifested determines the methods of channelling to be used. At a low level of manifested anointing, Jesus used the method of laying on of hands (Mark 6:5). At the beginning of His ministry, Jesus laid hands on everybody in a house meeting (Luke 4:40). Later in His ministry, as His fame increased and expectations and faith of the people grew, Jesus did not have to even lay hands (Mark 6:56; Matthew 14:36). Jesus' methods were determined by the faith level of people. For those who had the faith to receive without the need for laying on of hands, Jesus ministered accordingly (Matthew 8:8). It is interesting to note that Jesus had intended to personally minister when He said, *"I will come and heal him"* (Matthew 8:7). However, since the centurion's faith level was such that a spoken word would suffice, He ministered accordingly. We should therefore not be restricted to a stereotype method of ministering but we should flow with the level of anointing manifested. So when the strength of the anointing comes, then you can do many things with it. You must be careful that when you channel your anointing, your consciousness must be to impart a blessing. Not just for the phenomena but a tangible blessing. So it is a tangible force of anointing. And for that very reason different preachers have different styles. Whatever styles you have, you must watch that you do not just play games. But when you do play games you will not progress to the level of mighty miracles. I am talking about something very serious here. A lot of the people of God today are playing all these kinds of phenomena.

PRACTISING THE ANOINTING:

In the realm of the anointing, there is another dimension called *practising the anointing*. The anointing requires practice. In the natural, it is the same way. If you expect to be very good at music, you have to discipline yourself to sit down at those instruments and play it and practice. In the natural, practice makes perfect. In the spiritual, you also need practice to make the gifts of God perfect. You just have to practice it until you are accurate in your flow of the anointing of God. Faithfulness is a tremendous key to grow into the next level of the anointing that God has on our life. This helps us to move into a different phase of ministry that He has for our life. We have to be faithful in those areas. Just be faithful to fellowship with the Holy Spirit; get more Word into you; just be faithful to spend more time in praise and worship; just be faithful to spend more time in prayer. When you spend a lot of time before the face of God, you will build your spiritual voltage to the level where you could sense the tangibility of the anointing. We touch a point to cover those who do not seem to feel any manifestation of the anointing. When you reached a stage where you have a tangibility that is where we must recognize its tangibility and manifestation, pinpoint it, and understand what it is telling you. Then check yourself how it felt; what was it like; how did it come -it takes a lot of experimentations. These things that we learn you need to keep practicing them until it becomes a part of you. After several times you learn to recognize it. Learn to recognize its peculiar sensation in your life.

How Do I Practise The Anointing?

God could call you to operate in the measure of ten volts of anointing. As you move in your anointing, sometimes you find that you were not up to it. You did not spend enough time with God. Alternatively, the response from people to your ministry fluctuates. Sometimes they have more faith in you but sometimes they have less faith in the anointing that God has placed in your life. In some meeting, they have high expectancy but in some meetings low expectancy. *So in what way does practising the anointing benefit?* So, keep testing the anointing and it is through this process that you will get to understand the levels and dimensions you are operating in, how the congregation responds, the areas of improvement. You can stir or practice the anointing through the following spiritual exercises: **1.** Renewing your mind daily in His Word and His Will (Romans 12:2):*And be not conformed to this world: but be ye transformed by the renewing of your mind, that ye may prove what is that good, and acceptable, and perfect, will of God.* **2.** Meditating on His will and His Word continually (Romans 10:17): *So, then faith cometh by hearing, and hearing by the word of God.* **3.** Praying in the Holy Spirit (Jude 1:20): *But ye, beloved, building up yourselves on your most holy faith, praying in the Holy Ghost* **4.** Be sure that you have a relationship with Jesus (2 Corinthians 5:17): *Therefore if any man be in Christ, he is a new creature: old things are passed away; behold, all things are become new.* **5.** Living in Him must be your lifestyle. Most of all, it is abiding in Him, and He in You. The anointing comes from relationship (John 15:7). *If ye abide in me, and my words abide in you, ye shall ask what ye will, and it shall be done unto you.* **6.** Is everything you think, say or do welcoming the Holy Spirit's presence in your life? (1 Thessalonians 5:19) *Quench not the Spirit.* **7.** Check things out and hang onto the good, while resisting the evil. (1 Thessalonians 5:21) Prove all things; hold fast that which is good. (1 Thessalonians 5:22) Abstain from all appearance of evil. (1 Thessalonians 5:23) And the very God of peace sanctify you wholly. **8.** Spend time in His presence praising and worshipping Him. If only you could do this, you will provoke a torrential downpour of the anointing in measures you have never seen before.

Exercising your Faith in the anointing

We have to recognize how the anointing comes on our life. The interesting thing about teaching on the anointing is that the anointing is on one side and moving in faith is on another. We have to learn to move in both avenues. Sometimes it looks like moving in faith and moving in the anointing is diametrically opposed but they are not; they are complimentary to one another. That is why there is such a thing as *faith in the anointing*, meaning operating in the anointing through faith. If you preach the Word and tell the people not to go by their feeling but by the Word of God, you are ministering by faith. If you are ministering under the anointing, you cannot do that. You have to sense not with your five senses, not with your feelings, not with your mind, but with your spirit. You have to move into the realm of spiritual sensory perception where you would know the anointing peculiar and particular to you coming on you. The anointing we operate in is proportional to our faith level (Romans 12:6). A man full of faith is also full of power and anointing (Acts 6:5,8; 11:24). The reason the disciples could not tap on the anointing Jesus gave them to cast out a devil was because of their lack of faith (Matthew 10:1; 17:20). If we expect a baby Christian to grow beyond the faith level they received at conversion, then why do we expect a believer to remain at their first level of believer's anointing?

It is ridiculous especially when the anointing level is proportionate to the faith level. Moreover, the grace of God and the anointing of God are directly related. We can grow in grace (2 Peter 3:18). When we grow in grace we grow in the anointing of God. *Growth in glory produces an increase in the believer's anointing.* The glory of God and the anointing of God are directly related. When the anointing of God fills a place, the glory of God as a cloud is sometimes manifested (Exodus 40:34; 2 Chronicles 5:14). In fact it is the glory of God that causes people to fall under the power of the Holy Spirit. An increase in glory in our lives would definitely produce an increase in the anointing. Now if we are exhorted to grow from glory to glory, and since growing in glory produces growth in the anointing, then we should realize that we can grow in the anointing (2 Corinthians 3:18).

Deeper Revelations Of The anonting

ACCOMMODATING THE ANOINTING

In order to experience a greater manifestation of the anointing in your life, you need to create space and room for the anointing. Accommodating the anointing is an act of creating a conducive spiritual atmosphere and climate for the rain of the anointing to thrive, operate and precipitate over the masses. It means creating a viable platform and opportunity for the anointing to be manifested tangibly and visibly in the natural realm. In 1 Kings 4, the Shunamite woman created room for Elijah and by so doing it enabled Elijah to operate in miracles, signs and wonders even unto healing her son. When restricted or uninvited, the anointing might not work fully. That is why the bible says *whoever receives a prophetic received the prophetic reward. What is the prophetic reward?* It is the prophetic anointing. It can only operate when received, accommodated and a space created wide enough to allow the anointing to operate. Accommodating the anointing infers developing your capacity to contain the anointing. Some people's spirits are so under-developed such that even if the anointing comes in abundance, they are not capacitated to receive it. That is why Jude says in Jude 20 that *builds up your most Holy faith by praying in the Holy Ghost.* Praying in the Holy Ghost is one of the ways of enlarging your spiritual capacity so that you can contain the anointing. It is a pity that multitudes are not able to move in the anointing because they have not created enough space or room to contain the anointing. The greater truth is that the glory of God is immensely revealed where He is welcome. At times believers are so preoccupied with their empty church programmes and agendas such that they hardly create room for a deeper manifestation of the anointing. That should never be your portion.

MAINTAINING THE ANOINTING

There is such a key factor in the realm of the anointing called *maintaining the anointing*. Many ministers of God do not know how to maintain the anointing after they have received it. They would operate in the anointing for some time and then fizzle out. It is one thing to receive an anointing; yet it is another to maintain and increase it. The key to maintaining the anointing is a fasted life. The Lord wants to fill us with His power. He wants us to walk in His anointing so that He can pour out His love, His blessings, His compassion and His healing mercy over the world. For most Christians, receiving the anointing is not the problem; the challenge is *keeping* it. We receive the anointing when we come to Jesus in faith and repentance. The Holy Spirit comes to us and takes up permanent residence in our heart. As we learn to listen to and obey His voice, and as we are filled with the Spirit, we begin to see more and more of the evidence of the presence and increase of the anointing in our lives. This is not easy to keep it because it requires that we die to self. Only the smell of our burning flesh on the altars of our selfishness will release the full fragrance and potency of the anointing. We can't keep the anointing by hoarding it for ourselves. The only way to *keep* the anointing is to give it away. Keeping the anointing means learning to focus on the primary things. First of all, we need to focus on Jesus Christ. He is our Saviour, our Lord and our all in all. Focusing on Jesus means getting to know Him better and better and growing to love Him more and more.

Ministers must learn to walk in the anointing daily. We cannot expect that because we knew an anointing in God a few months or years back that we are automatically walking in the anointing now. It is true that the anointing abides, but we also must abide in the anointing! A "has-been" will not accomplish anything for God unless he first gets back into the flow of the anointing. We can all examine our own hearts in this area and need to continually so that nothing creeps in unawares and robs us of the fulfilment of the Holy Spirit in our lives. Remember Samson (Judges Chapters 13 to 16)? He knew the power of God's Spirit in a mighty way, but he drifted away to the point that he did not even know when the Spirit of God had departed from him! He did not recognize or discern the change taking place; he just "took it for granted" that God was still with him, but He wasn't. We must guard against the same apathy in our own hearts.

Secondly, we need to cultivate a personal relationship with the Holy Spirit. Get to know Him, welcome Him and drink daily and deeply of His water of life. The Holy Spirit is a Person. He is coexistent, coeternal and coequal with God. He is our Helper, Teacher, and Comforter. He is the Resident Lord of the Church. He gives spiritual gifts to empower and anoint you to reflect our glorious Bridegroom Jesus. He transforms us from glory to glory. One of the surest ways to diminish the power of the anointing in your life is to neglect your personal relationship with the Holy Spirit. We can grieve Him with our stubbornness, by gossip, by backbiting other Christians or by other misdirected words, actions or attitudes of the heart. Staying in tune with the Holy Spirit requires daily repentance –allowing the Holy Spirit to expose our thoughts and attitudes in His perfect light and turning to Him and His grace to transform us more and more into Christ's image.

The anointing is maintained by fasting and prayer. Fasting alone does not do much but fasting combined with prayer, or fasting combined with faith, releases tremendous spiritual resources. In modern civilizations, fasting is the act of releasing our consecration and expectation in God. Many tribal people would sometimes travel for days and weeks to reach an evangelistic or healing service. Their 'act' of walking and travelling is a release of their faith and expectation. In modern cities today, we travel to meetings by air-conditioned transportation and reach a meeting with less sacrifice than the tribal people. In tribal places, people come along when they are really keen or have high expectations (it would take high expectations to be willing to travel for days and weeks through the jungles) whereas in modern cities, people casually 'drop by' just to see what is going on. When the disciples asked Jesus why they could not cast out the demon, Jesus pointed to their unbelief (Matthew 17:20). His recommendation was that they fast and pray (Matthew 17:21). The disciples had received the power and authority to cast out demons. They had the ability. They had the anointing. Jesus knew that the anointing had waned in His disciples' lives and thus instructed them to fast and pray. Fasting and prayer are keys to maintaining the anointing of God in our lives. Fasting does not change God but it will definitely change us. Our spiritual hunger, visions and desires are intensified in a fast.

WALKING IN THE ANOINTING

It is imperative that we desire more than anything to continuously walk in the anointing. One thing I have learned is that receiving an anointing is very easy because in some cases people just receive it as an impartation from a man of God. However, in order to walk in the anointing, there is a price to pay, and it is a heavy price. To receive the anointing and to walk in it are two entirely different things. It must be understood that we neither run nor fly in the anointing but we walk in the anointing. Walking in the anointing implies taking practical steps to graduate from one level of the anointing to the other. Remember that the anointing is the second dimension of the supernatural realm. Therefore, in order for you to operate mightily in that realm, you must be first catapulted from faith *(first dimension)*, through the second dimension to the third dimension. It is of paramount significance to unveil the divine truth that if ever you want to harness the anointing of God from the supernatural realm, you better be in the spirit so that you can making a pulling on the anointing from that realm. Paul attests to this truth when he admonished us in Galatians. 5:16-19:

> *But I say, walk by the Spirit, and do not gratify the desires of the flesh. For the desires of the flesh are against the Spirit, and the desires of the Spirit are against the flesh; for these are opposed to each other to prevent you from doing*
> *what you would. But if you are led by the Spirit you are not under the law. If we live by the Spirit, let us also walk by the Spirit.*

It is worth highlighting the divine truth that there are different levels of being in the Spirit. A person can call him or herself Spirit filled but yet lives in the flesh. There are different levels of being in the Spirit and there are also things to do in order to keep being in the Spirit. However, it is disheartening to note that the vast majority of the church of Jesus Christ is not in the Spirit, hence they are not able to walk in the anointing. If the whole church of Jesus Christ is moving in the Spirit today, the whole world today will be shaken by what God is doing. I would rather say it this way. Most of the churches are in the Spirit some of the time. But only some in the church are in the Spirit all the time. And there is a certain realm in the Spirit that, that is there. We got to learn to flow with the Spirit in order that we may plunge ourselves into the greater depths of the anointing. Jesus Christ as He moved on this earth was always in the Spirit.

Being in the Spirit, living in the Spirit and walking in the realm of the Spirit is not as easy as people make it. A lot of people go in and out of that realm all the time. They say I am abiding in the vine. But most of the time they are pulling away from the vine and then coming on again. Then they ask Jesus, Jesus why do I not have fruit. You say that if I abide in the vine I will bear much fruit. Jesus says you are abiding some of the time but most of the time you are running around. Those little time that you have with Jesus, He would quickly channel all the nutrition to you so that you could bear fruit. And just as you got a few droplets you pulled off and you went aside again. No wonder it takes a long time to bear fruit.

TIMING IN THE ANOINTING

The next point that we have to understand is to know to be faithful to the timing for each level of anointing. Timing in the anointing implies having the ability to accurately project the next level of operation in the anointing. It involves accurately discerning when a greater measure of the anointing has been released for one to move to the next level and what to do when one gets to the new level. In the same way the sons of Issachar had an acute understanding of the times and seasons and new exactly what Israel ought to do, at a time, you can be catapulted to the realm of prophetic perception to accurately discern the timing of various phases of the anointing in your life.

Timing in the anointing involves operating in the right anointing, at the right time, in the right season at the right place and to the right (people) congregation.

In the case of David, the lion and bear were the testing but this one is different. It's the timing. Do you know that David had the power to conquer Israel during his seven years? He could have defeated them. He had an army that was stronger than the Israelites. The only reason he didn't do that was because he knew God didn't want him to do it. He waited and abided his time. Timing is important. When the people came it was the timing of God. He was anointed three times. First time by Samuel, second time by the tribe of Judah and third time by all of Israel. *David had three anointing.* And each time he moved into a different phase of ministry

As stipulated by His times and seasons, God does not do the same thing all the time. In order for us to be recipients of a torrential flow of His anointing, we therefore need to be sensitive to what He is doing at a particular time. Concerning the timing of the release of the anointing, God spoke through the Prophet Zechariah saying, *"Ask for me in the time of the latter rain and I will give you showers of rain."* In the context of this scripture, rain speaks of the anointing. The fact that God says we should ask for rain *during the time of rain* means it's not every time that it rains. God operates in times and seasons; hence if you ask for rain at such a time when it's not the season of rain, you will not receive much. It matters most when you ask for rain at the right time and God promises that when the correct timing is adhered to as per His calendar; the rain of power will come.

The law of timing implies doing the right thing at the right time. However, the truth is that at times people are doing the right thing but at the wrong time. A wrong timing might either result in a delay or procrastination of the anointing. The reason why many believers have not been able to receive a greater anointing despite the fact that they prayed and fasted is because of a lack of understanding of the law of timing. Unlike the sons of Issachar who had an acute understanding of times and seasons, hence knew what Israel ought to do at a particular time, many people do not understand or know God's timing yet it is such a critical determinant in matters of moving in the anointing. Timing is very important when it comes to matters of the miraculous because just like the sons of Issachar, you need an acute understanding of what to do, how to do it and when to do it with the anointing you have received because wrong timing might yield wrong results.

In a ministerial context, there is a time during a meeting whereby you can sense that the *cloud of the anointing* has been fully saturated. It is probably the best time to release the anointing upon the congregation. Sadly, many do not experience the spectacular display of the anointing because they are too quick to demonstrate the power of God when the river of God's anointing is not even flowing. On the extreme end of scale, there are those who get too stuck in their own church programmes and agendas such that by the time they finish and want to move in the anointing, the wave of power would have sailed by, leaving only a residue of God's presence. This is to tell you that you need to be sensitive when you are ministering so that you don't just demonstrate the anointing anyhow, but wait for that moment when the atmosphere is Heavenly pregnant with the glory of God. It is at that time that you can know that even angels are ready to release the glory of God in abundance, hence you may not waste any time but release the contents of Heaven right on the scene.

CHAPTER EIGHT

THE LEVELS OF THE ANOINTING

It is of paramount importance to unveil the divine truth that there are various levels or degrees of operation in the realm of the anointing. Therefore, in a ministerial context, we must be sensitive to the level and type of anointing flowing at each meeting so that we can be better instruments of the Holy Spirit. According to the word of God, every born-again, Spirit-filled child of God has a measure of the anointing in His life but every child of God is responsible for keeping and increasing that level of anointing. That is why some walk in a greater anointing than others. For example, some walk at the ankle level, some at the knee level, some at the waist level, and some swim in the deep at an overflow level. This is due to the degree they dwell in the presence of God and the extent to which they have cultivated the right spiritual atmosphere for the anointing to flow, the level of calling as well as the authority they command in the realm of the spirit. Greater levels of authority have been entrusted to the apostles and prophets, since they are the ones who walk in a stronger anointing and carry high levels of power. Every church or ministry who relates to the apostolic and prophetic ministries will also carry a strong anointing.

There are different ways of expressing the various levels of the anointing upon believers. In an endeavour to enhance a deeper or significant level of understanding of these levels, physical phenomena such as water, rivers, buildings or human vessels can be used to illustrate or demonstrate the concept of the anointing. This is because the bible says *that the things which are seen are a shadow or exact representation of the things which are not seen* (Hebrews 11:1). In the presentation of this revelation, three different classifications have been used to depict the levels of the anointing and illustrated with reference to the use of physical phenomenon *such as water, stature of a human vessel and the structure of a building.*

Frequency Revelator

THE FIRST TYPOLOGICAL CLASSIFICATION

USING THE POSTURE OF A HUMAN VESSEL

Ezekiel uses the physical phenomenon of water to demonstrate the various levels and degrees of the anointing. By so doing, Ezekiel's prophecy gives believers a clear picture of how the level of God's presence and power can increase in the lives of His people. In the context of this revelation, *water, streams and rivers* often refer to the presence and flow of God's Spirit. The highest attainable level of God's anointing is represented by the waters which flow from God's throne to individuals, groups or nations, and is often referred to as *the sea of the anointing*. Wherever these waters go, they bring healing and life to the needy. This implies that Spirit-filled believers have rivers of living water continuously flowing from their innermost being. Ezekiel gives a clear description of a five-fold level of the anointing upon every Spirit-filled believer. To cement this revelation with reference to a scriptural evidence Ezekiel gives us a narrative in which he says,

> *"Afterward he (the man with a measuring line) brought me again unto the door of the house; and, behold, waters issued out from under the threshold of the house eastward: for the forefront of the house stood toward the east, and the waters came down from under from the right side of the house, at the south side of the altar. Then brought he me out of the way of the gate northward, and led me about the way without unto the utter gate by the way that looked eastward; and, behold, there ran out waters on the right side. And when the man that had the line in his hand went forth eastward, he measured a thousand cubits, and he brought me through the waters;* THE WATERS WERE TO HIS ANKLES. *Again he measured a thousand, and brought me through the waters;* THE WATERS WERE TO THE KNEES. *Again the measured a thousand, and brought me through;* THE WATERS WERE TO THE LOINS. *Afterward he measured a thousand;* AND IT WAS A RIVER THAT I COULD NOT PASS OVER: *For the waters were raised, waters to swim in, a river that could not be passed over* (Ezekiel 47:1-9).

In the description of the anointing presented in the above mentioned scripture, Ezekiel reveals the FOUR LEVELS of spiritual maturity in the anointing. These are *ankle deep level, knee deep level, waste deep level and the overflow level.*

Deeper Revelations Of The anonting
LEVEL 1 - ANKLE DEEP ANOINTING

Ezekiel opened his narrative *in* Ezekiel 47:1 by saying that *"W hen the man that had the line in his hand went forth eastward, he measured a thousand cubits, and he brought me through the waters;* THE WATERS WERE BROUGHT UP TO HIS ANKLES. This speaks of *an ankle deep level anointing*. By description, an ankle is the lowest part of a human body which can only take you to a certain point and by the same token, the Ankle Deep level anointing speaks of the first or initial level of the anointing that is released within a believer at the beginning of the Christian Life. In other words, at new birth as an individual receives Jesus Christ into his spirit, there is a measure of the anointing that is planted or deposited within him as he begins the Christian journey or walk. This is the level of anointing which John spoke about when he said *But you have received an anointing from the Holy One and it abides within you* (1 John1:20). This is described by Bible scholars as the *believer's anointing* because *it* is available within every believer who has received Christ into their spirit. This level is for spiritual babes in Christ who still have to develop in their Christian walk.

However, the reality is that many believers only desire a shallow experience with God. Although they are saved and Spirit-filled, they seldom go beyond that point and still live a carnal existence, hence they are not in a position to affect anyone in their sphere of contact with the Gospel. To them, the baptism of the Holy Spirit is a once-off experience, thereafter, they seldom desire to migrate to higher levels of the anointing. Believers are therefore advised to graduate from this level of the anointing through a diligent study of the word, praying a lot in tongues so as to build yourself up as well as spending time in God's presence. By so doing, you will be able to grow quickly spiritually and sooner than expected, you will be ready to enter the next level of *the anointing*.

LEVEL 2 - KNEE DEEP ANOINTING

Ezekiel continues to describe his experience in Ezekiel 47:2 by *saying "Again he measured a thousand, and brought me through the waters;* THE WATERS WERE TO THE KNEES. This speaks of the knee deep *level anointing*. By description, the knee is slightly higher than the ankle and has the ability to bend and allow the body to perform diverse tasks. By the same token, the knee deep level of the anointing is not much greater than the ankle deep experience. However, it does indicate a deeper experience with God. The knee is connected to prayer, hence this level represents entering into this second level of the anointing whereby Christians are learning to pray and develop a prayer life and dependence upon the power of God. In essence, the knee represents prayer and could indicate a loyalty to the things of God, but at the same time believers at this level dare not wander deeper in the unknown realm of what God has for them. In the same way a knee can allow the body to bend and perform other functions, the knee level anointing has a potential to allow the believer to launch into higher territories in the anointing. However lack of experience in the realm of the anointing is what restricts the believer from treading on new grounds or invading newer territories in the realm of the anointing. Believers are admonished to migrate from this level through a deeper fellowship with the Holy Spirit.

LEVEL 3 - WAIST DEEP ANOINTING

In continuation, Ezekiel further records in (Ezekiel 47:3) *that Again the measured a thousand, and brought me through;* THE WATERS WERE BROUGHT UP TO THE WAIST. This speaks of a *waist level anointing*. By description, the waist is a central part of the body which has the ability to influence or determine the direction of other parts of the body. By the same token, the waist level anointing often refers to influence, hence at this level, the believer is beginning to use the anointing to influence those who are in his sphere of contact. This type of believer is active in the things of God and interacts with others around them. They may even have an active role in the local Church. They love the Lord and are somewhat involved in the activities of the ministry. But it does indicate an unwillingness to give everything. The waist measures half of the body length, indicating a half-hearted approach to full surrender. In other words, although they exhibit a significant level of commitment to church activities there are still certain things which they are holding on to. This is the point where Jesus refers to those who are lukewarm (Revelation 3:16) and also those who must make a choice to either submit everything to God or everything to the world (Mathew 6:24).

This level of the anointing can also be related to the armour of God spoken of in Ephesians. In Ephesians 6:14, the bible speaks of having girded your loins or waist with *truth*. According to (John 17:17), truth refers to The Word of God. This implies that at waist deep spiritual level, the believer grounds himself in good and sound doctrine. In other words, he is more enlightened in the word and starts to receive revelations. Moreover, the Loins represent the reproductive area. This implies that at the waist level anointing, as the believer gets established in the truth of God's word, he becomes reproductive through the anointing that dwells within him. In other words, the believer starts to produce the results of what the words of God talks about.

Deeper Revelations Of The anointing

LEVEL 4 - OVERFLOW OR FULLY-IMMERSED ANOINTING

Getting deeper with his revelation, Ezekiel continues in his narrative to report in Ezekiel 47:4 *that afterward he measured a thousand;* AND THE WATER WAS NOW A RIVER THAT I COULD NOT PASS OVER,
For the waters were risen, waters to swim in, a river that could not be passed over. This speaks of the *overflow anointing*. In the same way a body is fully immersed at this level, believers operating at this level of anointing are fully immersed or deeper into the Spirit such that they are led by the Spirit. Therefore, this is a level of deeper miracles, deeper revelations, deeper faith and everything which believers do in executed in greater depth. Moreover, this level of the overflow anointing is also a realm of supernatural manifestations and practical demonstrations of the Spirit and Power which Paul spoke about in (1 Corinthians 2:4) when he proclaimed that *he did not come with wise and persuasive words of human wisdom as he declared the testimony of Christ but with the demonstration of the Spirit and Power.* In other words, Paul operated in this realm hence he moved in greater dimensions of signs and wonders.

This level also represents a realm of great faith whereby the believer lives by faith and does not make decisions according to outward appearances, but has absolute faith in the Word and the Spirit. These believers are those who produce fruit, who are led by the Spirit (Romans 8:14) and are not influenced by the flesh or natural surroundings. They are a blessing to others, bringing light, hope, and joy and healing to those who are yoked in bondage. At this level of the anointing, the believers produce Kingdom fruit in their Christian walk and experience a breakthrough relationship with the Holy Spirit. Therefore this is a realm of signs and wonders where by the crippled are raised, the blind eyes are opened and incurable illnesses are healed. This level also represents a breakthrough point in the realm of the anointing. The believer literally swims through and is carried by the anointing in the same way Philip was carried by the tidal waves of the Spirit and was found in Azotus. It is a realm of transportation in the spirit, visitation to the throne room as believers begin to experience deeper spiritual encounters.

LEVEL 5: MEASURELESS ANOINTING

Ezekiel finally concludes his narrative by hinting that not only did the water turn out into the river but it also became a flood of waters flowing continuously in different directions. In Ezekiel 47:4, it says,

Son of man, hast thou seen this? Then he brought me, and caused me to return to the brink of the river. Now when I had returned, behold, at the bank of the river were very many trees on the one side and on the other. Then he said unto me, these waters issue out toward the east country, and go down into the desert, and go into the sea: the waters shall be healed. And it shall come to pass, that everything that lives, which moves in whichever river, shall live: and there shall be a very great multitude of fish, because these waters shall come: for they shall be healed; and everything shall live whither the river cometh."

This speaks of a *measureless anointing*. This is the level of the anointing at which Jesus operated or functioned under during his earthly ministry. The greater truth is that at this level of anointing, believers will do *greater works* than what Jesus did (John 14:12). This implies that now the Holy Spirit is sent without measure. The Holy Spirit has been sent in Acts 2 as prophesied without measure. He is now pouring out on all flesh. The potential is there for people to reach into that measureless anointing that Jesus had. Some people have moved in their respective office to a realm quite close to that. As they move into the anointing, they must move exactly as God shows them. No more and no less. There have been men and women who have moved into levels of anointing close to the level of Jesus Christ in the office God has called them. Every minister called by God should aspire to reach into that anointing without measure. It speaks of the believer flowing in the deeper things of God and the anointing. It is time to go deeper in the things of God and get into the spiritual waters of the anointing that require us to swim in.

It is at this level that the dead are raised, as there are mass resurrections experienced right across the Body of Christ. Believers have developed a significant level of maturity in the anointing such that they are able to channel it in the right direction to help the whole world. Therefore, believers at this level have the ability to launch the world into greater depths of the miraculous characterised by new waves of miracles, signs and wonders ever recorded in the bible. This is a realm of new manifestations because the anointing is so mature that it is able to create something new, a new dimension and a new experience. Creative miracles of glory are also experienced in this realm. This is a level of global manifestation and the rise of global visions that covers all the continents of the world in the same way the *waters issue out toward the east country, and go down into the desert, and go into the sea:* This speaks of global coverage and propagation of the gospel. This is the highest realm which all believers should aspire to attain in the realm of the anointing.

Deeper Revelations Of The anonting

THE SECOND TYPOLOGICAL CLASSIFICATION USING THE PHENOMENON OF WATER LEVELS

The Bible says there are three that bear witness on earth, the Holy Spirit, the Word of God, and the Blood of Jesus (1 John 5:8). These are the three witnesses that God uses to teach us all things. In the context of this scripture, the Apostle John used the word *"water"* many times in his writings, signifying *"the Word of God."* Throughout much of the Scriptures, God used natural things to teach us spiritual things. This is called *"figurative speaking, or symbolic language"* It is used to teach those who are in the natural realm, and who dwell so much in this lower plan of life, concerning how things are in the spirit realm. God relates many things to the natural realm while speaking of the spiritual realm. This is very important to understand, for we cannot know the things of the spiritual realm without knowledge of how God uses *"figurative speaking and symbolic language"* to teach us spiritual things. In 1 John 5:8, God is not speaking of *"liquid water."* God is speaking of spiritual things, not natural things. Natural things cannot change spiritual things. Natural things do not have any control over spiritual things. Spiritual things always have control over natural things. Even the Blood of Jesus, spoken of in 1 John 5:8 is not speaking of the liquid blood of Jesus. It is speaking of the *"life of the flesh that is in the blood."* By the same token, the anointing is figuratively demonstrated in the scriptures as a river of waters. Therefore, from this revelation flows three levels of the anointing which are ***well level anointing, river level anointing and rain level anointing.***

THE "WELL LEVEL" ANOINTING

It is the level of the indwelling presence of Holy Spirit in a person's life at the point of the new birth. It comes as an impartation upon an individual the instant he receives Christ into his life. The bible says on the last day of the feast, Jesus stood and cried out, saying, *"If anyone thirsts, let him come to Me and drink. He who believes in Me, as the Scripture has said, out of his heart will flow rivers of living water."* But this He spoke concerning the Spirit, whom those believing in Him would receive; for the Holy Spirit was not yet given, because Jesus was not yet glorified (Isaiah 55:1). In other words, Jesus spoke of this level of the anointing. It is described as a *well level* by virtue of the character of its manifestation. For example, it abodes in humanity and has not yet been provoked into manifestation because of the level of spiritual maturity of the believer at this stage. In the same way the water in a well is still, static, motionless or stable, this anointing also inhabits in humanity is a still, tranquil manner because it has not yet been activated, stirred because the believer is still new in Spiritual matters. In simpler terms, this is a measure of the anointing that has potential but it has not yet been tapped or activated. In the same way a well keeps the waters and does not spill it over, a believer at the well level anointing just keeps the anointing and does nothing about activating it to work in diverse situations.

The "river level" anointing

This level occurs at the point of the Baptism of the Holy Spirit. The Baptism of the Holy Spirit is the initiation into spiritual depth. It brings about identification with God. The difference between the well level anointing and the river level anointing is that the well level anointing takes place at *new birth* while the river level anointing takes place during *baptism in the Holy Ghost* which are two different experiences in the Spirit. *New birth* is there to initiate a believer into the Christian realm while baptism in the Holy Ghost is there to launch the believer into greater depths on the Christian realm. The reason why it is called a *river level anointing* is because of the character of its manifestation. In other words, unlike a well level anointing, this anointing does not stay stagnant; instead, it has a tendency to flow or ooze out of a human vessel. This is because at this level, the believer has learnt how to tap into spiritual principles to provoke or awaken the anointing into manifestation, hence it flows out in the same way a river flows. At this level, a believer has reached a certain level of maturity in the anointing such that he uses it to confront situations and circumstances. And as he speaks to poverty, sickness, disease and devils, the anointing flows out like a river to engulf, erode and food whatever obstacles lie on his way. One key characteristic of a river is that it erodes anything that stands on its way and this is the exact character of manifestation of the anointing at this level.

Moreover, one of the distinct characteristics of rivers is that they tend to make deposits along their journey. In the same way a river carries material and unreservedly deposit anywhere it goes, believers at this level of river anointing have learnt to fully commit, sacrifice and unreservedly give themselves to the work of ministry. Therefore you can't be at the river level anointing and still be selfish. The anointing is not for you, but for others. Increase can't happen in the life of a selfish person. Moreover, both wells and rivers are subject to *"climatic"* changes. By the same token both the well level and river anointing are subject to regulation by the Holy Ghost. However, association is what determines whether or not your *"well"* and *"river"* are full.

The "rain level" anointing

It is a greater truth that both the well and the river are subject to the rain. This means that if you want your well and river to be full, you must have rain. That is why the bible says *Ask the LORD for rain in the time of the latter rain. The LORD will make flashing clouds; He will give them showers of rain, Grass in the field for everyone* (Zechariah 10:1). God promised to rain His power on His people. God has promised a storm of anointing. Rain is symbolic of the release of God's power. God's anointing makes performance possible. Pray to God for rain—it's time for the spring rain! Ask God for rain and He will give it. The rain level anointing comes after the Baptism of the Holy Spirit occurs.

The Bible says as Peter began to speak the word, the Holy Ghost fell upon all those who had the word. In other words, there was a rain of the anointing that was falling upon the people at the instant the word was preached. Moreover, this anointing is best described by the experiences of the apostles during the early church as they prayed, *And now, O Lord, hear their threats, and give us, your servants, and great boldness in preaching your word. Stretch out your hand with healing power; may miraculous signs and wonders be done through the name of your holy servant Jesus." After this prayer, the meeting place was shaken, and they were all filled with the Holy Spirit. Then they preached the word of God with boldness.* The disciples had already been baptized in the Holy Spirit but when power of God showed up, and they all spoke in tongues. In other words, because of the rain of God's glory which manifested itself in the physical realm as an earthquake that shook the foundations of the house, believers received a doze of the anointing. The anointing is what fills the water levels in your life.

THE THIRD TYPOLOGICAL CLASSIFICATION

USING THE STRUCTURE OF A BUILDING

The typological illustration of a structure of a house can be used to illustrate different levels of the anointing or different stages through which believers graduate in the realm of the anointing. In the same way a builder of a house starts with a foundation, then builds a wall and concludes by putting a roof, believers in the realm of the anointing starts at foundation level then they graduate into a wall level and finally reaches the roof level which marks the highest level of spiritual maturity in the realm of the anointing. The greater truth is that we grow from one level of the anointing to the other and in the same way it is not possible for a foundation, wall and roof to be laid within a day, it is also not possible for one to build up the measureless anointing within a day. Instead, we grow progressively through these levels as we spend time in the word and fellowship with the Holy Spirit.

FOUNDATION LEVEL ANOINTING

The foundation level anointing is an anointing which lays a strong and unshakable foundation in your Christian walk with God. In other words, it establishes your character in God in the same way a foundation establishes the whole house. It establishes you in the word and in faith. It is called a *foundational level anointing* because it is the initial anointing which a person receives at salvation that lays a foundation in a believer's life. It comes as a measure of anointing in the same way one receives a measure of faith at new birth. That is why John says *you have an anointing form the Holy one and it dwells within you.*(1 John 2:20). However, one must not stay at this level for ever because it is just to provide the basics. In the same way a house that stays at foundation level will have problems; an individual who stays at foundational level of the anointing will not grow in his Christian life. When disciples met, the foundation of the house where they met was shaken. This implies that there is such a thing as the *foundational anointing* and at this level, the anointing you receive will work in the area of establishing you in the ministry.

WALL LEVEL ANOINTING

In the same way a wall anchors the whole building, the wall level anointing builds you, it anchors you. The anointing is there to build up your faith in the word. It is a *building anointing*. The bible says *when we pray in tongues, we build up our faith* and this is the same way in which the anointing is built at this level. The *wall level anointing* comes as we mature in Christ and have learnt the benefits of praying in tongues. At this level believers are able to make a significant impact in the spirit realm. God said to Jeremiah *I have made you an iron pillar and a bronze wall that no one will be able to stand against* (Jeremiah 1:18). There is a dimension in the anointing whereby God anchors you like a wall such that no one can resist you. This is the anointing that protects us during spiritual warfare. Just like a wall, the anointing spreads out to reach new territories in the spirit dimension.

ROOF LEVEL ANOINTING

At this level, the anointing covers you in the same way a roof covers the whole house. At this level, the anointing has grown and developed so much that is becomes a permanent *spiritual covering* in the same way a roof provides

Deeper Revelations Of The anonting

a covering for a building. There is a certain level of anointing that covers or protects you. At this level, you don't even have to fight against anything for the anointing covers you. It is a covering anointing, which is a mantle. Therefore, the roof level speaks of the development of the anointing into a mantle. At this level, one has such a governmental anointing which gives him greater authority to oversee, commands and directs other ministries in the body of Christ and literally control the whole world with God's power. Moreover, in the same way a roof stands out to distinguish a house from others in the neighbourhood, at this level, the anointing distinguishes you from the rest, it separates you from others. At this level, the anointing advertises you and makes you popular in the kingdom

CHAPTER TEN

LIMITATIONS OF THE ANOINTING

It is of paramount significance to highlight in this section the fact that the anointing has certain boundaries within which we operate. That the means when we move into the anointing, there are certain boundaries that God has set. We are free to move within those boundaries but not outside of them set by God for His anointing. Therefore, you have to learn the limitations of the anointing that can hinder you from flowing in it. If we don't recognise those limitations, we move outside of it, hence there may be repercussions. There are limitations by anointing; limitation by geography and limitations by office. If you move beyond that, you endanger yourself but if you move within your limitations, you magnify your ministry to the fullness. The following are limitations of operating in the realm of the anointing:

The type and nature of calling and office

There is a limitation in moving in the anointing that comes as a result of the call, the nature of assignment and the office within which one is operating. The limit that God set for you might be different from the limit God has set on another person. And they have to be faithful to their own limitations. God may have called you to go to a hundred nations and at the same time He may have called another person to go to ten nations. Therefore you need to know your limitation because there is a danger if you don't know your limitations in that you tend to be doing things that are not anointed. For example, when God calls you to be a prophet, don't try to be a teacher and if He calls you to be a pastor don't try to be an evangelist and if He calls you to be an evangelist, you don't try to be a pastor. You must learn to be faithful to what God calls you to do. Trouble starts when those who are not called try to do the work of those who are called. We must know

Deeper Revelations Of The anonting

where the boundary lines are and not cross them. God doesn't want all of us to be Jack-of-all-trades; instead, He wants us all to flow in the gift and call God has set for you. We have a few cases of people in the Bible that crossed those boundaries like King Saul. He was a king and when he tried to do the priest work, God rejected him. In the New Testament, it looks like you get away with it longer. But you don't get away with it in the end. The limitations that you have crossed will cost your very down fall. You don't get away with moving out of the office of God that He has set you in. He has placed you there, so don't move out. Remember if you are in the office in whatever role or position in any church, you are not there to serve men. You are there to work with men or women of God or to be a blessing. It is recorded in 2 Kings 18:1 that,

It came to pass in the third year of Hoshea the son of Elah, king of Israel, that Hezekiah the son of Ahaz, king of Judah, began to reign. And while he was reigning, Sennacherib came and surrounded King Hezekiah. When King Hezekiah heard, that he tore his clothes, covered himself with sackcloth, and went into the house of the Lord. Then he sent Eliakim, who was over the household, Shebna the scribe, and the elders of the priests, covered with sackcloth, to Isaiah he prophet, the son of Amoz.

Hezekiah was a King but he was not a prophet. In a time of trouble, Hezekiah is an interesting figure. He stood in one office but he was one of those who knew how to co-operate with the other offices. He established the priesthood again. He rebuilt the temple. That means that he helped to establish another office and put it in its rightful perspective. Why? Because he had secular power as a king. So he restored the priesthood. But even though he was powerful, he recognized the line that he cannot cross. When it came to the prophetic realm, he sent messengers to Isaiah who is a prophet and he received the word from the Lord. Here is where you see the co-operation of priests, kings, and prophets. Isaiah received the word of the Lord in 2 Kings 19:5:

So, the servants of King Hezekiah came to Isaiah. And Isaiah said to them, "Thus you shall say to your master, thus says the Lord. Do not be afraid of the words which you have heard, with which the servants of the king of Assyria have blasphemed Me. Surely I will send a spirit upon him, and he shall hear a rumour and return to his own land; and I will cause him to fall by the sword in his own land.

This is a tremendous incident here. Because of the fact that king Hezekiah cooperated with Isaiah the prophet, together they brought deliverance to Israel. You may not think much about that but let me say this word of assurance in a crisis is a great comfort. Hezekiah had no word from the Lord. He was a good king. He was faithful to his office as king and he brought prosperity to Israel. In that situation, he needed a prophet's word and even when he reached the end of his role, he relied on another ministry, another prophet. He is a king relying on a prophet to bring about the word of the Lord that will bring comfort to the Israelites. This is not the first time. There are several times he did it. Which is why I see the humility of Hezekiah. In his humility, you know where your limitations are and you don't go beyond it. You know the limitations of your call and your office.

Free Will

The anointing of God never bypasses the free will of man. In other words, you may desire to minister the anointing to a person but if he or she does not desire it, there is no way that you could force the anointing on him or her. This is one of the limitations that free will imposes on an anointing. Strangely, when the person is in the presence of the anointing, the anointing can work something in him or her just by being present there. Like in Kathryn Kuhlman's meetings, a lot of people were healed who never went there for healing. So, the question in people's mind is:

How come God healed them when they haven't even gone through the basic laws of asking, seeking, and praying. Remember the laws of the anointing work differently from the laws of personal faith. The law of personal faith requires asking, seeking and praying. The laws of anointing operate differently. The fact that the person was in the meeting indicates a choice. Whether they were dragged there, compelled or whatever way was used but their being in the meeting had an effect. But of course we assume that the majority of those people were highly persuaded to be there. Without the persistence of those who brought them they may never be there. The reason is the anointing will not violate the free will of the recipient.

The second factor is the one who ministers the anointing. The one who ministers the anointing also has a free will too. Let's say you operate in prophecy. No matter how much the anointing that comes on your life and you receive the word of prophecy, the Holy Spirit will not make you walk to the front of the stage to give the word of prophecy. He will not ask you to do it. He will impress you to do it. He will persuade you to do it. But He will not force you to do it. I have a free will as to obey God or not. I have a free will whether I want to listen to what the Spirit is saying to do and obey or not. Sometimes you don't feel like you want to obey because some of the

Deeper Revelations Of The anointing

instructions are not quite that easy to follow. I mean if one day the anointing comes upon your life and the Holy Spirit says, *"Spit on his eyes."* So if I don't want to obey it's my free choice. And the anointing will not work. The anointing respects the free choice that we have. If anyone operates in the anointing that bypasses his free choice and makes him do things without his free choice and will, that person is not of God. He is like a demon-possessed person who lost his free choice.

William Branham prayed for people who got healed. But sometimes he would say, *"You must go and in three days you are to get baptized in water and your healing will be completed and retained."* It is a test of obedience. If the person failed to follow through, he would lose his healing and the whole process stopped. When Jesus said, "Go, show yourself to the priest", do you know they could not be forced? They could decide to go the next day and it may affect the anointing of God. Elisha told Gehazi to take a rod and go and lay it on the dead son of the widow. He was told not to greet anyone along the way. Gehazi carrying the staff had a free choice to talk or not to talk. He was not forced not to talk. He had a free choice and he still could talk. So when a person does not want the anointing, there is no way the anointing can be forced upon him. They must want it. They must choose it.

The anointing is subject to a person's free will, it will not bypass the free will. If for example, you are afraid and do not want to fall under the power. You made a mental decision that you do not want to fall under the power. I say most probably you will not. You have blocked yourself out of the manifestation. This doesn't mean that everybody must fall under the power but since you made a mental decision not to fall, the anointing will respect your free choice and you won't fall. God will not bypass your volition. You just blocked the manifestation of the Holy Spirit. God will honour your free choice. If you say, *"Lord, I do not ever want to prophesy,"* even though the gift may come to your life and stir in your spirit, there is no way it's going to flow through you. Mentally you have made a choice not to exercise the gift. If you have made a choice saying, *"Lord, I will obey you only in this method,"* straightaway you blocked out all other methods but the one method you have chosen. So the anointing is limited by our free choice. That is why you must deal with your free choice to open yourselves to say, *"Lord, anyway, anyhow, whatever you want to do."* We yield our free choice. We yield our will to God so that God could use us to the maximum possible and not be limited in any way.

Those prophets Isaiah and Ezekiel may seem crazy to the world but to me I know that they are obedient. I admire them because if God gave me the same instructions I may never be as obedient. Think about this instruction that God gave, *"Go and shave your head bald."* How many of you will do it. God says, *"Go and play with the mud and make a city of England."* Who will do it? God says, *"Take your clothes and bury it in the sand in the sight of everybody."* Then God says, *"Go and dig it up again."* God says, *"Wear it,"* and you wear it. And there was Isaiah who walked naked for three years saying, *"Thus said the Lord."* This is very hard instruction. But, yet mentally having shut those things out God will never work in your life. That is Old Covenant but the New Covenant has some interesting things that if we shut our mind and our free will off, we stop God from working. We have to open our free will to God. So this is what I call the limitation of the free will.

In Mark 5:17 after Jesus healed the demon possessed man, it says then they began to plea with Him to depart from their region. That's marvellous because Jesus went there to preach the gospel to them. Later on you read in the gospel of Mark chapter 6 towards the ending that Jesus went back to that region. But when Jesus originally went there, all the people on their free choice told Him not to come. Is it God's will for Jesus to go there? Yes. Otherwise Jesus wouldn't head there. Don't think Jesus went there just to deliver that man and go home. We know that is not true because later in Mark chapter 6 He went to the same place again. It was the perfect will of God for Jesus to enter into the area of Gadarenes to preach the gospel. But because the people rejected Him, do you think Jesus will go against their free will? He never. He went with their free will and He went back. He went home because they didn't want Jesus. Free choice was involved

The nature of Operation

The other limitation concerns the operation of the anointing. For example, if God calls you to operate in visions, then you must be faithful. But if God never called you to operate that way, don't attempt to copycat someone who does. You have to be faithful to the method God has chosen for you. When Kathryn Kuhlman starts operating in her style, Oral Roberts came to her meeting and admitted to her that God never asked him to operate that way. But when Oral Roberts ministers, he has to lay his hand on every person. That is his special operation. See God sometimes calls a man with a message and a method. God has not limited me to a method. But for some people God limits them to a method. Do you know William Branham was also limited to a certain method? He had to use his left hand to hold a person to discern. Sometimes it would break into other people where he could call them out. But he will always use his left hand and when he move his left hand he will know exactly what is wrong. God sometimes calls a man or woman with a message and a method. If God gives you a methodology that He says, *"This is your special operation,"* please don't change it. God likes you the way you are. Even no matter how hard you try to imitate another person's anointing by the outward way, you won't have it. God limits a person to a certain operation. As you flow along remember the limits of the operation that will open onto you.

However, the operation can change with time and season as you progress at each phase in your ministry. Kathryn Kuhlman will never lay hands when she operates. She requires quietness. Benny Hinn with the same type of anointing needs the same thing he wants you to be quiet. Learn to flow with each preacher's anointing. It is their limitations of their operation. If they don't have it they cannot flow. That is their pattern and method that God ordains for them to flow with. At the same time I would like a certain atmosphere of reverence. But I don't require pin drop silence to operate in the gifts. What I am talking about is the method that God requires a person to use. Flow with it because that person may be limited to that operation. If they don't have that they cannot operate. They are limited to the mode of operation.

Lack of a godly character and integrity

To maintain the anointing, we need to have godly character and integrity. God can limit the flow of your anointing to your character. It's very hard to say which came first. Sometimes it's very hard for us to tell whether it's the character that changes because of the anointing or it's the anointing that is flowing with that person's character. The funny thing is that when you start moving in the anointing after a long time, the characteristic of the anointing that is required becomes a part of you. In the natural realm and in the spiritual, there is a pattern. We understand that the anointing can come irrespective of character. But certain types of anointing require a change in character. If you were as timid as a mouse and you are called to be an evangelist and soul winner, you have got to overcome your timidity. You may say *I am not that character*. You have no choice. If you are called and if you say you are not going to change then the anointing cannot flow in your life. You have to be very outgoing.

Frequency Revelator

And for some of us, we maybe in an area where our character limits us from public speak. You may never have spoken. But if God calls you to be a teacher to the body of Christ, you are going to start somewhere and it may be harder to start because of that. But somehow you have to break it and let it become a part of you. So, there is what I call *limitations of character.* Think about the apostle Paul. He was one of the most educated men in his days brought up at the feet of Gamaliel, a Pharisee of the Pharisee, a well-educated, top man, but God sent him to the barbarians. You wouldn't send him to the Gentiles. The Gentiles in those days were called barbarians. And the Jews here they are educated and God called this Peter who always engages his mouth before he thinks; loud speaking, brash in his habit, uncultured in his style, fisherman, man in the street, talk rough, and yet God sent him to the most educated. Here is fisherman proclaiming the gospel to doctors of the law. As of Paul, God sent a doctor of the law to the barbarians. Strange are the ways of God. So, don't interpret your character to mean that's where His call is. There are limitations of character that we must understand. We must overcome some areas of our character in order to facilitate the anointing through our lives. In some areas, we must develop a new character in God. What we are not in ourselves we have to change until the day comes you are so conformed you are the call and the call is you. When people look at you, you feel exactly into the mould that God made you to be your part in the body. Our character had to change and conform to that which God so desire.

The body

Then we come to the limitations of the body. Our body is not a new body yet. We must realize that no matter how anointed you are or how much God uses you, our body has a limitation. Even Jesus in John 4 felt tired. In John 4:6, Jesus being wearied from His journey, sat thus by the well. Jesus had a physical body that felt tired. And in His Gethsemane experience in Mathew 26:43 He came and found His disciples asleep again, for their eyes were heavy. I want you to notice this in verse 40 and 41. He asked them *"Why are you asleep, can't you watch with Me?"* At other times, when you are tired and the work is fnished, you need to rest. In fact one of the miracles of feeding of the fve thousand was when Jesus said let us go to rest. He wanted to rest. He wanted to get some time away from the crowd because there is much coming and going. And the crowd followed them. We need to know when to rest. There are limitations of the body. In the book of Philippians 2, Epaphroditus because of the work of Christ he came close to death. In other words, he over worked himself and he nearly died.

Deeper Revelations Of The anonting

When it's the time to rest you need to learn how to rest. Do you know that there were some people who are so active whether in business or in ministry who don't know how to sleep? They need pills to sleep because they are so highly strung and stressed. We got to learn how to rest our body properly. Sometimes men or women of God with wonderful ministries die prematurely because they don't know how to take care of their body. No matter how greatly God use you, remember your limitations of your physical body. And in the 1950s a lot of people with great anointing fell. But some men and women of God pushed themselves beyond natural. Although the anointing will sustain you, it will sustain you to a certain extent and you have to use your common sense and wisdom. Beyond it, God is not going to protect you if you deliberately overwork your bodies. I had to learn the hard way because sometimes I minister so much I hardly get time to catch up on my reading here and there. So, sometimes after all those hectic times of ministry, I just sit down and read. Why? That's my hobby and at the same time I want to learn, I want to grow. Some people tend to either overwork or underwork their bodies. If you have never pushed your body to the limit you do not know what a versatile body God has given you. There are limitations but you have to check yourself if it is your own zeal that has been overdone.

Unbelief/lack of faith

The anointing can be limited by unbelief. In Mark 6:6, *Jesus marvelled because of their unbelief.* Then He went about the villages in a circuit teaching. It tells us in Mark 6 that Jesus could not do any mighty work because of their unbelief. So the anointing is limited to people's faith level. Do you know one reason why the Holy Spirit could work so many miracles through Kathryn Kuhlman? It is because by the time people came, their faith level was built up. The majority of people attend church just for teaching and as a result you get proportionally what they came for. Your expectation and faith level limits the anointing that is able to flow. The
Bible records in Mark 6:53 that,

> *When they came out of the boat, immediately the people recognized Him, ran through the whole surrounding region, and began to carry about on beds those who were sick to wherever they heard He was. Wherever He entered, into villages, cities, or country, they laid the sick in the marketplaces, and begged Him that they might just touch the hem of His garment. And as many as touched He was made well.*

Notice the faith level was so high. How high was it? The moment He landed, they saw Jesus and quickly they ran and got the sick people. Why? They expected the sick to be healed. Their faith level was now higher. We have to have faith in God as well as a measure of faith in the instrument of God. We have to tap on the anointing upon.

Now, here is the area where I want to show why the anointing of God works very high like in the Thessalonians. In 1 Thessalonians 1:5, Paul says *For our gospel did not come to you in word only, but also in power, and in the Holy Spirit and in much assurance, as you know what kind of men we were among you for your sake.* Look at that the gospel came with power. Why did it come with power because in I Thessalonians 2:13 it says *For this reason we also thank God without ceasing, because when you received the word of God which you heard from us, you welcomed it not as the word of men, but as it is in truth, the word of God, which also effectively works in you who believe.* In other words, we not only have to respect God's words but we have to respect the instrument that God brings when they are obedient. When Jesus came into His hometown they asked, *"Is this not the carpenter?"* They were not prepared to receive Jesus as a Messiah. They were only prepared to receive Him as an ordinary carpenter. Because they had no respect for the instrument, they did not receive the anointing. We have to have as much faith.

Don't forget that it was still Paul who said, *"Follow me as I follow Christ."* That means Paul is saying as he is imitating Christ you still can take him as a role model. So, we need to realize that everyone still needs a role model that they could build their life upon. People still need mentors to move and pattern their lives and then move on from there. We don't want to limit ourselves to a person but yet we start somewhere. We have to start somewhere to build in our lives. One of the reasons why the anointing moved so powerfully in Acts 5 was because they began to esteem the instrument of God higher than before. Look at Acts 5:15 that even the shadow of Peter passing by might fall on some of them. Now look at verse 13 don forget without verse 13 you cannot get verse 15. Verse 13 yet none of the rest dared join them, but the people esteemed them highly. It didn't say that they esteemed God highly of course they do. But they not only esteemed God now they began to esteem His vessel. When people says to have faith in God but don't have faith in the vessel of God they have locked themselves up. People who talk that way do not know how to tap on the anointing. And they can be in the presence of anointing and because they don't regard the man of God as a man of God they get nothing. They blocked themselves from the anointing of God. You've got to have faith in the man of God as well as faith in God to receive from the man of God.

Deeper Revelations Of The anonting

When William Branham ministered, he would always ask, *"Do you receive me as a prophet of God?"* You know why he is asking that? You have to have faith in him too. In his book, *"I Believe in Visions,"* Kenneth Hagin recounted his first vision where Jesus placed the anointing of God on his palm. Jesus said,

"You must tell them what I have done for you. You must tell them I have appeared to you. I have put a coal of fire on your hand and I touched your hand and gave you a healing anointing and if they believe what you said they will tap on the anointing."

Do you know that you have to believe in the man of God? Do you know one of the ways the devil discredits men of God who are faithful is by highlighting the sins of men of God who have failed? So that today people have less faith in men of God because they saw one or two fall.

Lack of fellowship with the Holy Spirit

It must be understood that the Holy Spirit is the source and originator of the anointing. In other words, He is the one who personally administers the anointing and rubs it on human vessels. Fellowshipping with the Holy Spirit connote to the act of developing deep intimacy and sensitivity to His voice, leadings and promptings. It is when your spirit gets so infused and mingled with the Spirit of God such that you are one in spirit. This is what we describe in metaphorical language as the *drinking together of spirits*. It is during these sacred moments in the presence of God that greater volumes of the anointing are imparted and rubbed onto your spirit and transformed into the likeness of Christ Jesus and Heavenly secrets are unveiled to you. Therefore, anybody who doesn't fellowship intimately and deeply with the Holy Ghost forfeits the opportunity to have greater volumes or measures of the anointing rubbed on him. The only reason some men and women of God fall is that they give less time to prayer and the Word. Before a person falls, they start neglecting prayer, the fellowship of the Holy Spirit and meditation on the Word. If you keep these tools strong all the time, you are immovable. I could name every one of them who have fallen and I can tell you the price they paid to get the anointing. Some of them were proven and tested. Finally, the anointing came and with the anointing, came success. Then they did not have enough Word and prayer in their life and intimacy with the Holy Spirit that with time, they lost the anointing.

Religion, man-inspired teachings and misconstrued doctrines of your past

Misconstrued traditional teachings can be a major stumbling block to operating in the anointing. The devil will use the wrong teachings implanted in your mind as certification to block these types of anointing from flowing in your life and ministry. It might take time to undo the wrong teachings in your mind and heart. If you do not give yourself fully for the Holy Spirit to teach you, your mind and heart will be a major block to these new types of anointing that the Holy Spirit has prepared for the end times. Therefore, some people will not be able to tap into greater dimensions of the anointing because of wrong teachings or bad theology. Some people are very sceptical about the new move of God. They have a tendency to view manifestations with suspicion, hence they find it difficult to easily accept them. This might also limit you from moving in the new wave of the anointing. If God is moving and you don't move with Him, you are left behind. This is how many believers have failed to tap into the greater anointing which God is releasing over the Body of Christian this end time season.

PRAYER FOR IMPARTATION OF THE ANOINTING

Heavenly Father, in the Name of Jesus Christ, I thank you for the depth of revelations of your Word encapsulated into this writing. I believe your Word and embrace these revelations for my season. I believe that I'm catapulted into the realm of the anointing. I therefore receive an impartation of the overflow anointing from you into my spirit, right now. By faith I believe I have received and now I'm rightly positioned and ready to propagate the world with the anointing of the Holy Ghost. I unapologetically declare that I am the world's most anointed man/woman. I am saturated with high volumes of the anointing, I'm submerged into greater depths of the anointing, and I'm filled to the brink of full capacity with the measureless anointing of the Holy Ghost; my cup runeth over. By reason of the anointing no sickness, darkness, neither evil nor power can stand on my way. As the breaking forth of the waters, so does the anointing upon me breakthrough in every sphere of life. Thank you for making me such a wonder in this world and a miracle worker to launch the world into greater depths of the miraculous. I ascribe unto thee all the glory, Honour and Power due your name.

Amen!!

*Congratulations!
And Welcome to the league of The Anointed!*

PRAYER FOR SALVATION

If you have never received Jesus Christ as your Lord and Personal saviour, loudly recite the following prayer, now:

> *Dear Heavenly Father! I present my life before you today. I confess with my mouth that Jesus Christ is Lord and believe in my heart that He died on the cross and was raised from the dead after 3 days, for the remission of my sins. I acknowledge that I'm a sinner and ask you to forgive me for all the sins I have ever committed. Wash me with the precious blood of Jesus Christ and write my name in the Book of life. I therefore receive eternal life into my spirit right now. I declare that from henceforth, Jesus Christ is my Lord and Saviour and I proclaim His Lorship over every area of my life. Thank you Lord Jesus Christ for saving my soul. I'm now a child of God, born again, born of the Spirit of the living God.*

Amen!

Congratulations and Welcome to the family of God. You are now a brand new creation that belongs to the lineage of the blessed, the Royal priesthood, the Chosen generation and the highly favoured! Most importantly, you have now received the most precious possession of Heaven, the anointing of the Holy Spirit, glory to Jesus!

AUTHOR'S PROFILE

Frequency Revelator is an apostle, called by God through His grace to minister the Gospel of the Lord Jesus Christ to all the nations of the world. He is a television minister, lecturer and gifted author, whose writings are Holy Ghost breathings that unveil consistent streams of fresh revelations straight from the Throne Room of Heaven. He is the president, founder and vision bearer of Frequency Revelator Ministries (FRM), a worldwide multiracial ministry that encompasses a myriad of movements with divine visions such as Resurrection Embassy *(The Global Church)*, Christ Resurrection Movement (CRM) *(a Global movement for raising the dead)*, the Global Apostolic & Prophetic Network (GAP) (a *Network of apostles, prophets and fivefold ministers across the globe*), Revival For Southern Africa (REFOSA) *(a Regional power-packed vision for Southern Africa)* and the Global Destiny Publishing House (GDP) *(the Ministry's publishing company)*. The primary vision of this global ministry is to propagate the resurrection power of Christ from the Throne Room of Heaven to the extreme ends of the world and to launch the world into the greater depths of the miraculous. It is for this reason that Frequency Revelator Ministries (FRM) drives divergent apostolic and prophetic ministry visions and spiritual programmes such as the Global School of Resurrection (GSR), Global Resurrection Centre (GRC), the Global Healing Centre (GHC), Global School of Miracles, Signs and Wonders (SMSW), Global School of Kingdom Millionaires (SKM), Global Campus Ministry as well as Resurrection Conferences, Seminars and Training Centers. To fulfil its global mandate of soul winning, the ministry spearheads the Heavens' Broadcasting Commission (HBC) on television, a strategic ministerial initiative that broadcasts ministry programmes via the Dead Raising Channel *(a.k.a Resurrection TV)* and other Christian Television networks around the world.

Presiding over a global network of apostolic and prophetic visions, Apostle Frequency Revelator considers universities, colleges, high schools and other centers of learning as critical in fulfilling God's purpose and reaching the world for Christ, especially in this end-time season. As a Signs and Wonders Movement, the ministry hosts training sessions at the Global School of Resurrection (GSR) which includes but not limited to, impartation and activation of the gifts of the Spirit, prophetic declaration and ministration, invocations of open visions, angelic encounters and Throne Room visitations, revelational teachings, coaching and mentorship

Frequency Revelator

as well as Holy Ghost ministerial training sessions on how to practically raise the dead. This global ministry is therefore characterized by a deep revelation of God's word accompanied by a practical demonstration of God's power through miracles, signs and wonders manifested in raising cripples from wheel chairs, opening the eyes of the blind, unlocking the speech of the dumb, blasting off the ears of the deaf and raising the dead, as a manifestation of the finished works of the cross by the Lord Jesus Christ. The ministry is also punctuated with a plethora of manifestations of the wealth of Heaven through miracle money, coupled with the golden rain of gold dust, silver stones, supernatural oil and a torrent of creative miracles such as the development of the original blue print of body parts on bodily territories where they previously did not exist, germination of hair on bald heads, weight loss and gain, as well as instantaneous healings from HIV/AIDS, cancer, diabetes and every manner of sickness and disease which doctors have declared as incurable.

The author has written a collection of **42** anointed books, which include *The Realm of Power to Raise the Dead, How to become a Kingdom Millionaire, Deeper Revelations of The Anointing, Practical Demonstrations of The Anointing, How to Operate in the Realm of the Miraculous, The Realm of Glory, Unveiling the Mystery of Miracle Money, New Revelations of Faith, A Divine Revelation of the Supernatural Realm, The Prophetic Move of the Holy Spirit in the Contemporary Global Arena, The Ministry of Angels in the World Today, Kingdom Spiritual Laws and Principles, Divine Rights and Privileges of a Believer, Keys to Unlocking the Supernatural, The Prophetic Dimension, The Dynamics of God's Word, The Practice of God's Presence, Times of Refreshing and Restoration, The Power of Praying in the Throne Room, Understanding Times And Seasons In God's Calendar, How To Defeat The Spirit Of Witchcraft, The Practice Of God's Presence, 21 Ways Of How To Hear God's Voice Clearly, Miracles, Signs And Wonders, Understanding Prophetic Dreams And Visions, Deeper Revelations Of The Glory Realm, The Prophetic Significance Of Gold Dust, Silver Stones, Diamonds And Other Precious Stones, The Power Of The Apostolic Anointing, Deeper Revelations Of The Five-Fold Ministry, The Anatomy And Physiology Of The Anointing, How To Activate And Fully Exercise The Gifts Of The Spirit, Healing Rains, The Realm Of Love, The Revelation Of Jesus, The Second Coming Of Jesus and Rain of Revelations,* which is a daily devotional concordance comprising a yearly record of 365 fresh revelations straight from the Throne Room of God.

Apostle Frequency Revelator resides in South Africa and he is a graduate of Fort Hare University, where his ministry took off. However, as a global minister, his ministry incorporates prophecy, deliverance and miracle healing crusades in the United Kingdom (UK), Southern Africa,

Deeper Revelations Of The anonting

India, Australia, USA, Canada and a dense network of ministry visions that covers the rest of the world. As a custodian of God's resurrection power, the apostle has been given a divine mandate from Heaven to raise a new breed of Apostles, Prophets, Pastors, Evangelists, Teachers, Kingdom Millionaires and Miracle Workers (*Dead raisers*) who shall propagate the world with the gospel of the Lord Jesus Christ and practically demonstrate His resurrection power through miracles, signs and wonders manifested in raising people from the dead, thereby launching the world in to the greater depths of the miraculous. To that effect, a conducive platform is therefore enacted for global impartation, mentorship, training and equipping ministers of the gospel for the work of ministry. Notable is the realization that the ministry ushers a new wave of signs and wonders that catapults the Body of Christ into higher realms of glory in which raising the dead is a common occurrence and demonstrating the viscosity of the glory of God in a visible and tangible manner is the order of the day. Having been mightily used by God to raise the dead, in this book, Apostle Frequency Revelator presents a practical model of how one can tap into the realm of God's resurrection power to raise the dead, impact the nations of the world and usher an unprecedented avalanche of billions of souls into the Kingdom, Glory to Jesus! May His Name be gloried, praised and honored forever more!

Frequency Revelator

AUTHOR'S CONTACT INFORMATION

To know more about the ministry of Apostle Frequency Revelator, his publications, revelational teachings, global seminars, ministry schools, ministry products and Global missions, contact:

Apostle Frequency Revelator

@ Resurrection Embassy

(The Global Church)

Powered by Christ Resurrection Movement (CRM)

(Contact us in South Africa, United Kingdom, USA, Germany, Canada, Australia, India, Holland & Other nations of the world).

As a Global Vision, The Ministry of Apostle Frequency Revelator is present in all the continents of the World. You may contact us from any part of the world so that we can refer you to the Resident Ministry Pastors and Associates in respective nations. Our offices and those of the ministry's publishing company (Global Destiny Publishing House (GDP House), are ready to dispatch any books requested from any part of the world.

Email:
frequency.revelator@gmail.com

Publisher@globaldestinypublishers.com

Cell phone:

+27622436745

Deeper Revelations Of The anonting

+27797921646

Website:

www.globaldestinypublishers.com

Social Media Contacts:

The Author is also accessible on Social media via Facebook, twitter, instagram, YouTube, and other latest forms of social networks, as Apostle Frequency Revelator. For direct communication with the Apostle, you may invite him on Facebook and read his daily posts. You may also watch Apostle Frequency Revelator on the Dead Raising Channel a.k.a Resurrection TV and other Christian Television channels in your area

Christian products:

You may also purchase DVDs, CDs, MP3s and possibly order all of the 21 anointed books published by Apostle Frequency Revelator, either as hard cover books or e-books. E-books are available on amazon.com, Baines & Nobles, create space, Kalahari.net and other e-book sites. You may also buy them directly from the author@ www.gdphouse.co.za. You may also request a collection of all powerful, revelational teachings by Apostle Frequency Revelator and we will promptly deliver them to you.

Ministry Networks & Partnerships:

If you want to partner with Apostle Frequency Revelator in executing this Global vision, partnership is available through divergent apostolic and prophetic ministry visions and spiritual programmes such as the Global School of Resurrection (GSR), Christ Resurrection Movement (CRM), Resurrection TV (a.k.a The Dead Raising Channel), the Global Apostolic & Prophetic Network (GAP), Global Resurrection Centre (GRC), the Global Healing Centre (GHC), Global School of Miracles, Signs and Wonders (SMSW), School of Kingdom Millionaires (SKM), Global Campus Ministry and other avenues. By partnering with Apostle Frequency Revelator, you are in a way joining hands with God's vision and thus setting yourself up for a life of increase, acceleration and superabundance.

AUTHOR'S GLOBAL MISSIONS, PARTNERSHIPS & COLLABORATIONS:

If it happens that you are catapulted into the realm of demonstrating the anointing following the reading of this book, please share your testimony with Apostle Frequency Revelator at the contacts above, so that you can strengthen other believers' faith in God all around the world. Your testimony will also be included in the next edition of this book.

If you want to invite Apostle Frequency Revelator to your church, city or community to come and spearhead Resurrection Seminars, Conferences, Dead Raising Training Sessions or conduct a Global School of Resurrection (GSR), whether in (Europe, Australia, Canada, USA, South America, Asia or Africa), you are welcome to do so.

If you want to start a Resurrection Centre or establish the Global School of Resurrection (GSR) in your church, city or community under this movement, you are also welcome to do so. We will be more than willing to send Copies of this book to whichever continent you live.

If you want your church or ministry to be part of the Christ Resurrection Movement (CRM) and join the bandwagon of raising the dead all around the world, you are welcome to be part of this Heaven-ordained commission.

If you want more copies of this book so that you can use them in your church for seminars, teachings, conferences, cell groups and global distribution, please don't hesitate to contact Apostle Frequency Revelator so that he can send the copies to whichever continent you are. Upon completion of this book, you may also visit www.amazon.com and under the "Book Review Section," write a brief review, commenting on how this book has impacted your life. This is meant to encourage readership by other believers all around the world.

Deeper Revelations Of The anonting

If you want to donate or give freely to advance this global vision, you may also do so via our ministry website (www.globaldestinypublishers.com) or contact us at the details provided above. If you need a spiritual covering, impartation or mentorship for your Church or ministry as led by the Holy Spirit, you are welcome to contact us and join the league of dead-raising pastors that we are already mentoring in all continents of the world.

If you have a burning message that you would like to share with the whole world and you would want Apostle Frequency Revelator to help you turn your divine ideas and revelations into script and publish your first book, don't hesitate to contact us and submit a draft of your manuscript at the Global Destiny Publishing House (www.globaldestinypublishers.com). We will thoroughly polish your script and turn it into an amazing book filled with Throne Room revelations that will impact millions across the globe, glory to Jesus!

The Lord Jesus Christ is coming back soon!

Made in the USA
Middletown, DE
29 January 2020